CLOCKWINDER
Who Wouldn't Say No

BY THE SAME AUTHOR

Commons Knowledge (Seren, 1997)
Baglu 'Mlaen (Gwasg Gwynedd, 1998)
Dragons Led by Poodles (Politico's Publishing, 1999)
The Unusual Suspect (Biteback Publishing, 2010)
How to be an MP (Biteback Publishing, 2012)

CLOCKWINDER
Who Wouldn't Say No
THE LIFE OF DAVID TAYLOR MP

PAUL FLYNN

Biteback Publishing

First published in Great Britain in 2012 by
Biteback Publishing Ltd
Westminster Tower
3 Albert Embankment
London SE1 7SP
Copyright © Paul Flynn 2012

Internal images pages 1, 2, 3 and 6 © The Taylor family, page 4
© David Bennett and pages 5, 7 and 8 © The *Leicester Mercury*.

Every reasonable effort has been made to trace copyright holders
of material reproduced in this book, but if any have been
inadvertently overlooked the publishers would be glad to
hear from them.

ISBN 978-1-84954-221-0

10 9 8 7 6 5 4 3 2 1

A CIP catalogue record for this book is available from the
British Library.

Printed and bound in Great Britain by
CPI Group (UK) Ltd, Croydon CR0 4YY

CONTENTS

FOREWORD BY SPEAKER
JOHN BERCOW

I was delighted to be asked to provide a foreword for Paul Flynn's excellent biography of our sadly missed colleague, David Taylor.

David was an extraordinarily diligent parliamentarian – every working day he could be found in his place on the back benches poised to probe and scrutinise the government without fear or favour. He was a superb questioner with an unrivalled ability to use the English language to construct witty, pithy and often devastating questions both on behalf of his constituents and on wider issues affecting the country. Indeed, his last question in the Chamber was on the security of people in Northern Ireland – a long way from his Leicestershire seat. David was also an assiduous contributor to debates in Westminster Hall, the House's second Chamber, where he demonstrated his interest in a very wide variety of issues. He joined the Speaker's Panel of Chairs in 2005 and proved to be an effective referee, as well as a brilliant player.

On a personal level, I remember David as a principled, conscientious man who was a passionate supporter of, but never a slave to, his party. He was an excellent example of a fearless, independent-minded and articulate member of the House. He was also a committed family man and it is indeed a great tragedy for all of us that we lost him when he had so much more to give. It is fitting that such a fine parliamentarian's life has been written by another excellent, and like-minded member, Paul Flynn, and it is to his credit that he has given so much of his time and passion to tell David's story.

ACKNOWLEDGEMENTS

The House magazine asked me to write an obituary of David Taylor in January 2010. The only part of David Taylor's story that I knew then was his parliamentary life. He was a trusted friend whose talents I admired. To understand David's life before and outside Parliament I needed help. David's family and friends have been very generous with their time and very open in providing me with stories of the David Taylor I did not know.

He came to Parliament with a rich hinterland as a councillor, accountant, computer expert, polymath and a convinced Christian socialist. My grateful thanks to all those who have shared their memories with me: his wife Pamela, daughters Rachel, Sarah, Jessica and Catherine, sister Margaret Martin, journalist Lee Marlow and friends Canon David Jennings, David Drew, Alan Costello, David and Alison Bennett, David Farmer, Richard Smith, David Wragg, Ross Willmott and former staff Lauren Otter, Daniel Crimes and Matt Mulley. The *Leicester Mercury* and David Bennett kindly allowed me to use their splendid photographs.

Hollie Teague of Biteback Publishing was immensely helpful and a source of sound counsel. I am also deeply indebted to Lisa Eynon, Jayne Bryant, Sam Flynn, Ruth Winstone and Robyn Wall who devoted their great skills, time and advice to the creative process. Any deficiencies are mine.

TAYLOR'S LAW

Anger is never without an argument.
It is rarely a good one.

Why destroy Baghdad in order to save it?

Acquiescence on crime facts can be guilt by default.

Benefits do not allow people to fall
back on cushioned indolence.

PFI is financial illiteracy raised to an art form.

Steer a line between mindless obedience
and persistent rebellion.

An MP can choose the weather for a few days a year.

The Tory government had more leaks
than a Rhondda vegetable show.

An election? Draw the curtains
and don't answer the door!

'Do-able' means a non-zero prospect
of anything happening.

Opencast? Once bitten, twice shy, thrice defiant.

Is it forever the fate of football fans to
be fleeced by flaky foreign financiers?

I'm a mushy peas socialist rather
than guacamole Labour.

Government new IT is exorbitantly expensive,
utterly unreliable and lamentably late.

If it weren't for the last minute,
nothing would ever get done.

PREFACE: DEATH
AT CHRISTMAS

'The MP for North West Leicestershire, David Taylor, has died.'
    The BBC report struck like a thunderbolt in the Christmas holiday of 2009.

David was a fit, trim, non-smoking, non-drinking cyclist and cricket player who was never ill. It was a bereavement that no one anticipated. This tribute to David asks whether an MP caught up in the parliamentary expenses scandal was 'killed by the *Daily Telegraph*'.

Did the wholly justified public anger punish indiscriminately the guilty and the innocent? While I know I am swimming against the tide of public opinion a start must be made on telling the full truth of that screaming living nightmare which afflicted the British political class.

The more I learn about David's life, the more I admire him. But, this is not a hagiography. David was a man not a saint. He had his foibles and failings – many of which were endearing. He had no ambition to be a minister or a statesperson. He used his energy, humour and idealism to serve his constituents. My new book of advice, *How to be an MP*, is dedicated to David Taylor, 'the best of us'.

MPs seeking a model life to emulate will find it within these pages.

PRECOCIOUS BOY

In the heart of England, in the spaces between working class and middle class, between war and peace and between his older sister Margaret and his younger sister Susan, David Leslie Taylor was born on 22 August 1946.

It was a good time for the birth of a socialist. The most successful Labour government had been in office for twelve months. They were busy pioneering a generous welfare state and the National Health Service. The miners in David's home village of Heather were embarking on an era of pride and prosperity as their status had never been higher. The mines were about to be nationalised. The privations of war were a fading memory. It was a time of hope. A brave new world of fairness and solidarity was being created. Optimism was rampant. The influences that were to shape David Taylor's remarkable future nurtured him.

In public life David appreciated the novelty value of recalling that the place of his birth was the exotically named Ashby-de-la-Zouch. That was the site of the local hospital. His home and his heart were in the village of Heather – his cherished habitat which he described sixty years later as the place where 'the proud working-class mining culture thrived and still survives'.

His idyllic family childhood was tinged with the sadness of his younger sister's lifelong health problems. His elder sister Margaret fondly recalls the love of two talented, literate and highly intelligent parents. They turned to French when it was 'pas devant les enfants'. Later they communicated in Latin after the sharp-witted David and Margaret adroitly recognised simple French.

David's father, Leslie, came to Leicestershire from Newcastle upon Tyne in circumstances that remain a mystery. A family upset is thought to have prompted his move to the Midlands. Some tantalising details are known. He was the son of Alderman Swainson Taylor. They were a prosperous family who, in 1901, employed a driver, a maid and a gardener.

Leslie was the second oldest of four brothers; Edwin, Rodney and Evelyn completed the quartet. David's mother knew little about her husband's family. It was never discussed and the children were not encouraged to ask questions. David's sister Margaret explained:

> My father's family was never mentioned. Then we had a message that his mother had died. A case was packed and he went away to the funeral. Father came back with his French prize that he had won in the Royal Grammar School, Newcastle in 1914. Next thing we knew, we had a visit from Dad's brother. Uncle Rodney was a delightful guy who had taken over the family business.

He looked at the situation in our council house with our utility furniture. A few days later a huge furniture van delivered a beautiful hand-carved sideboard, an oil painting and some elegant silver spoons. Uncle Rodney came to the area on business. He always came for a meal. He would also send the family five-shilling postal orders to prop up the family finances.

Leslie was a complex, troubled and vulnerable individual – idealist, nervous and secretive. Haunting memories of the First World War plagued him. His soldier's life was very similar to that of my father. Both were machine gunners. They were despised as the lepers of the battlefields. The firmly held belief was that British and German soldiers vowed that machine gunners would be shot and never taken as prisoners. It was vengeance for the thousands of troops who were 'slain like cattle' by the machine gunners. The experience ruined my father's life. He suffered wounds and a tobacco-addiction cancer that killed him at the age of forty-three. Leslie Taylor never talked about the horrors he witnessed. He could not control the depth of his emotions on Armistice Days when he openly wept. He spared his family the terrible images of the hell of the trenches that tormented him.

His peacetime work was in the then Ministry of Labour allocating civilian jobs to the returning soldiers and discharged prisoners. He was seen as a 'fine gentleman' and spoke the received English of his day, which impressed the folk of Middle England. His Newcastle accent was apparent only when he was stirred by anger

or affection. He called Margaret his 'bonny lass' in the
warm tones of Tyneside.

Leslie met Eileen Fowkes in Nottingham. She was
nineteen years his junior. Eileen had proved that she
was a capable worker who was judged the second most
proficient in the country as a shorthand typist. This
was one of the few skilled jobs then open to women.
She was a brilliantly intelligent woman. A generation
later, her talents could have flowered in many other
more demanding and satisfying jobs. This was an
epoch when meritocracy was in embryo – especially for
women. In spite of the new opportunities created by
the new Labour government, Eileen's children Margaret
and David were fated to suffer similar life-restricting
lost chances.

HEATHER BORN

Early family life was spent in a flat in Leicester and then sharing with an aunt. 'Living in rooms' was normal for that time. Today they would be classed as 'under-housed' or 'homeless'. Only those with memories of the cramped housing conditions of the early post-war years can appreciate fully the triumph of gaining the key to a new council house. It was a sumptuous gift of light, space, a large separate kitchen and a bathroom plus the luxury of an indoor toilet. The Taylor family were the first tenants of a splendid four-bedroomed house in the new estate of Sparkenhoe, Heather. It is now owned by them and is still the home of David's younger sister Susan.

Mediaeval England was divided into parcels of land named 'hundreds'. 'Sparkenhoe' was one of them; its name meaning a gorse knoll of land. Heather was listed in the Domesday Book of 1086 as Hadre, meaning heathland. Sparkenhoe fulfilled the high ambitions of the 1945 Labour government to replace cramped Victorian hovels with spacious, airy and well-equipped homes with large gardens. Wise political leadership has maintained the desirability of living in the unspoilt now mixed-tenured community of Sparkenhoe. The fine council house was an object of great pride to the Taylor family.

The superficially homogenous village of Heather had its subtle class divisions. The working-class miners' families were devotees of the Wesleyan Chapel and the middle-class professionals and farmers worshipped at St John the Baptist Church. There is another up and down to the village. The Crown is known as the top pub; the Queen's Head is the bottom pub. The Crown is on a slight rise and is about a foot or two higher above sea level than the Queen's Head. From such trifles social divisions emerge.

From his early years the young boy David impressed. It was obvious to all that David was exceptionally intelligent. He delighted his parents and teachers who were convinced that his future would be brilliant. The extraordinary power of his memory was a rare gift. The Heather village school had old Victorian 'standards' not classes. David was always ahead of his chronological age and he reached the top standard at about the age of eight. He was precocious throughout his school life.

Early signs of a politician's guile and competitiveness were also apparent. A lifelong friend of David's told me that when they were about five or six years old they played marbles in his parents' garden. He said:

If my marble appeared to be going into the hole David would run alongside it and deflect it away. There was consternation when games of ludo or snakes and ladders went wrong for David. He would throw a tantrum. There was real rivalry between us in collecting foreign stamps. If I had a delivery of stamps in the post it would be followed by a bigger delivery for David.

David recalled the starry-eyed romance of stamp collecting in his writings in 2008:

> My mother was a village postwoman for thirty years, so delivering the post was much part and parcel of my everyday life. And it seemed almost miraculous in those pre-Internet, pre-satellite TV, pre-texting days that for a few old pence, a sticky little bit of perforated paper could whisk a letter or package to wherever you wanted it to go – another community, another country or another continent.
>
> Stamp collecting was a very popular hobby. Most children's comics would carry adverts for businesses like Broadway Approvals who, on receipt of your written request, would send you a free Penny Red or an instant collection of world stamps along with a book of stamps for sale. You chose what you wanted from these 'approvals' and sent the rest back together with a postal order for the value of the ones you had bought.

David's overdeveloped competitiveness was a lifelong trait that later propelled him to high achievements in science, politics, computer programming and community service. But sometimes ambition was trumped by caution. On one occasion he lost his zest to be first, as another school friend recalled:

We had regular visits from the school dentist. He was a
very frightening man. His wife was his receptionist and
she was even more terrifying. We were due to see the
dentist in the Wesleyan Chapel. That afternoon David
did not make it. He was discovered cowering under a
bush in a nearby field.

That was the last example known of David avoiding
a challenge.

His inventiveness was apparent from an early age.
There was even a hint of sharp practice to achieve one
boyhood ambition. When David was very young his
grandfather Roland ran the post office. In each jar of
Robertson's jam there was a paper golliwog between
the lid and the greaseproof covering. Those prodigious
jam-eaters who collected the full set were rewarded
with a prized enamel badge. Roland allowed David
and his friend to delicately prise open the jam-jar lids
to find the rarest gollies. The common examples were
skilfully replaced so that the skulduggery was invisible
to the eventual purchasers. David bought the jam that
contained the rare gollies. It was a matter of great kudos
for David to flaunt his enamel badge on one of his Fair
Isle pullovers, which were his trademark apparel.

David's maternal family roots ran deeply in Heather.
His mother's father was the postmaster and her grandfather had come on a pony and trap from Derbyshire to
become the first postmaster in the village in the 1930s.
He lived to the age of ninety-eight, proving the long-
life quality of the family's genes. It was an element that

was part of the later speculation on the cause of David's premature death.

Home life revolved around the post office, which was also the village general store. It was both a prestigious middle-class occupation and an albatross. Margaret recalls that her mother did not have a single day off work for decades. One solitary visit to Skegness is fondly recalled. It was organised with immense difficulty.

The ambience of childhood determined the pattern of David's DNA. Many years later he used his platform in Westminster to say:

> I'll do everything I can to safeguard the Royal Mail services to its customers and to look after the interests of our local posties because delivering is in my blood, from going round with my mum as a child to umpteen campaigns, leaflets and newsletters as a politician. And in all that time I have only had the misfortune to be bitten by dogs twice!

An accident cast a long shadow over the lives of the whole family. The freak Lynmouth disaster in January 1952 shocked the nation. A wall of water swept through the Devon villages drowning thirty-four sleeping people. The Taylor family reacted to troubles in the way they always did: with practical compassion. Helping others was the core of their family's life and David's heightened sense of civic virtue became a lifelong trait. While collecting contributions for the disaster fund door-to-door in Heather, David's father Leslie tripped over a wire while crossing from one garden to another and broke his collarbone. He was then fifty-three. He never worked again. It was a heavy emotional and financial blow. He had always had a nervous temperament and the injury left him debilitated. A very heavy smoker, he was doomed to a life of deepening disability and permanent financial problems.

The powerful solidarity of the mining village eased the financial hardships through some practical barter. Eileen was an accomplished knitter and David was proud to flaunt the best collection of Fair Isle pullovers in the village. Eileen supplied other families with winter woollies. In return, an open coalhouse door was a signal of an unmet need. Without a word being said a delivery of coal would arrive. Uncle Rodney helped and added to his occasional postal orders. He gave the family interest on a £1,000 war loan.

The mature David had happy memories of his childhood:

I do recollect wonderful trips to the cinema with my mother and two sisters back in that two-TV-channel era of the 1950s. We might not have had CGI graphics or booming stereo surround sound, but when the lights went down and the projector began to whir, we were transported to lands and times far beyond our somewhat austere post-war existence here in the towns and villages of North West Leicestershire.

Who can forget biblical miracles happening before our very eyes when Charlton Heston as Moses in *The Ten Commandments* parted the Red Sea with a wave of his staff and the majestic line, in a deep baritone, 'Behold His mighty hand'? As did Ibstock – the village Palace being where I first encountered the magic of the silver screen.

He was to remain a happy romantic for the rest of his days.

WIGGIE'S PROGRESS

David was popular at school because of his pleasant manner and his sporting prowess. He always had hair that was longer than fashion demanded. That doomed him to the nickname of 'Wiggie'. David eccentrically had fond memories of school dinners and waxed lyrically and nostalgically about them in 2000: 'My favourite school meal was made up of two things I haven't had for years – steak and kidney pudding followed by chocolate blancmange topped with cornflakes.' Parliamentary cuisine must have been a disappointment to him. Never have I seen cornflake-topped blancmange on the menu in the Commons Members' Dining Room.

Gifted David left Heather primary school for Ashby Boys' Grammar School two years early. It may have been a disservice to him. He enjoyed the early recognition of his abilities but David was mixing with boys who were physically two years more developed than he was.

Academically David continued to race ahead, passing his O levels at fourteen and his A levels at sixteen. Then education stopped: the family's finances did not run to university places. Margaret and David were well qualified to benefit from higher education. Both later regretted missing the chances that were enjoyed by their less able friends. Meritocracy was dawning but not quickly enough to give Margaret and David the early opportunities they deserved.

When his own daughters attended university, David recalled:

> I know from personal experience what it's like to leave school at sixteen with A levels and pass up the prospect of becoming an undergraduate because of family circumstances. Like thousands of others there simply wasn't enough money around to let me take a degree at that time. I did follow the hard road of a part-time degree much later.

Their father's illness was the main reason that they were denied university places. Both were Oxbridge material. One oddity was David's failure to pass English literature at O level. It always rankled with him. His command of written and spoken English was exemplary and added distinction to his future careers. David later compensated for the lost opportunity. He strove in Parliament for a fair comprehensive education system for all. A tabloid once stupidly criticised him for attacking the grammar school system that he had enjoyed. It was unjust criticism. He won his place at a grammar school. There was no other way forward then for a bright underprivileged child. David was attacking the double standards of opportunity that divides a later generation.

David's father lived on his reduced pension until

his death from emphysema in 1968 at the age of sixty-nine. His heavy smoking was a major contributor to his demise and he suffered from breathing difficulties. David later recalled, 'My father died from a smoking-related illness after years of smoking heavily. I experienced at first-hand what happens to a family when they lose someone so precious to them. It's a terrible thing and it sticks with you forever.'

His mother Eileen was then forty-nine and the family faced formidable financial problems. Margaret remembers the day in March 1968 when David called with the sad news: 'Dad has died.' Margaret and David did the calculations and realised that it would be difficult to cope financially. The link with Uncle Rodney and the interest paid on the war loan ended, but Rodney gave Margaret, David and Susan £1,000 each. David used his to buy a white van – not a status symbol but a liberating means of discovering the beautiful Leicestershire countryside. Cars became a lifelong fascination to him.

Margaret is proud of her mother's response to the penury of her husband's death. She paid a heartfelt tribute:

What I admired her for was that she literally got on her bike. She became the village post lady, a job she did magnificently until she retired in 1987 at the age of sixty-eight. Two post ladies on their bikes then served the village. They were replaced with a man in a van. When the snow fell the following winter, no post turned up. They all said, 'When Eileen and Edna were delivering we always had post. Every day.'

Eileen lived to see her son enter Parliament. She was immensely proud of his achievement, but she fretted when he did not always obey the Whip. Conformity and obedience were features of her character. She admired David for having his own point of view. He paid a loving tribute at her eightieth birthday party in 1999. Eileen had lived a full life of devoted service to her family and her village. It was a ceaseless task. She rarely had a day off work. She never had a passport or visited France to try out her impressive language skills. She was proud and at ease that her idealism, strong work ethic and Christian values had helped shape the personality of one of the best backbench MPs of his generation. She lived to bask in the shining glory of the first six years of his parliamentary career and the warm approval of the Heather folk. She died in 2003.

PUPPY TRAINING

David and Margaret recovered after the university door was slammed in their faces. They both built strong careers. David gained an Open University degree in Maths and Computing in 1974 and began his thirty-year stint in local government.

His brilliance shone. He was a prizewinner in the Institute of Municipal Treasurers and Accountants final exams. But his image was far removed from the conventional dark suit and tie of the ambitious local government officer on the promotion trail. A colleague recalls his 'slovenly' appearance and cavalier attitude to authority. It would have been a struggle for him to give unlimited respect to those of his 'superiors' who possessed less than one-quarter of his intelligence. 'At the end of the time of every lecture, irrespective of whether the lecturer had finished or not, David would put his jacket on, then his scarf, then his overcoat. Then he glowered at the lecturer until he stopped.'

His council colleagues spoke warmly of David's lack of airs and graces. They said he never flaunted his mental agility and creativity. He just had natural ability. In the late 1960s he moved from the accountancy profession to computing. He wrote the software for a successful computer program named CASCAID (Careers Advisory Service Computer Aid), which aided school leavers with their career choices. The program developed into a commercial success and a profit-making enterprise for the council. It was complex and innovative and evolved into the modern-day Kudos and Adult Direction programs. It is still in use now by many councils throughout the UK. One of my staff enjoyed using Kudos in her Swansea comprehensive school in the 1990s.

David was well placed for a meteoric career in the emerging world of computing. He made no money from the commercial success of CASCAID and Kudos. Others did. Establishing a business of his own based on his inventive talents could have been a soaring commercial and financial success. But making money never really captured his interest. It was a lifelong trait that was not understood by those who later falsely accused him of acting for mercenary reasons. His interests and ambitions were more elevated. He was acquisitive for efficiency, progress and justice.

One of the great disappointments of his life was his failure to be promoted to the head of the council's computer department. He was superbly qualified. Office gossip put it down to his unorthodox idiosyncratic appearance and behaviour. Friends recall that his eating and dressing habits were unusual. He was a keen runner and in the changing rooms afterwards he would shower and then have dinner in the canteen. His method of dressing was different to everyone else.

It was claimed that he would begin dressing by putting on his socks and his shoes first. His novel eating habits are still the subject of some fascination. He would have a main course and a sweet, but he always ate his sweet first 'because it would get cold'.

David was indifferent to his appearance. His close friend, former miner Alan Costello, said: 'If you took him to the best tailor in the country, he'd look a mess. When he came to a barbecue he had a pin-striped suit on, when he went to a do at 10 Downing Street his clothes were right for a barbecue.' Wearing red socks in London was an obsession. They were not necessarily matching ones. He felt no nominative pressure to live up to the promise of sartorial elegance of his surname.

His untidy appearance did not detract from his appeal to his future wife, Pamela Caunt. Pamela was born in Loughborough and her father's family lived in the ancient village of Quorn. After David had moved from the staffing section of Leicestershire County Council into the accountancy section, Pamela was employed in his old department. It was a great stroke of luck. Romance blossomed and they were married in September 1969.

Pamela could not recall whether David had any previous girlfriends. If there were any they were not of any significance. Even the excessive demands of political life and its enforced absences placed no unbearable strains on this settled marriage. Their meeting in the unromantic ambience of a council office was the spur to a happy shared life together.

They first lived with David's mother. In the forty years of their marriage they set up home in three separate houses on Main Street, Heather. Pamela says it was 'a very happy marriage'. They were blessed with four beautiful daughters, Rachel, Sarah, Jessica and Catherine, who gave them great happiness. Baby David was born after Sarah but he lived for only a few hours. It was suggested to me that the loss of the infant boy influenced David's views on the value of healthcare and abortion. Pamela does not agree.

Pamela was a Labour supporter but not as passionately devoted as David. He joined the Labour Party for the first time shortly after the wedding. He soon became deeply involved in parish council politics. His motivation was the devastation of his square mile by pit closures and the new ugly deserts created by opencast. There were seven pits in the area when David was a young man. They have all gone.

The seasoned Labour Party campaigner Alan Costello recalls his first meeting with the man he called 'Dave'. Alan greeted him as a 'young pup, wet behind the ears' when they first met. He took David by the hand and 'showed him how to canvass'. Alan had the right to be patronising to the new Labour Party member. He had spent a lifetime in the Ellistown Mine, which closed in 1989. His father had been a Labour councillor and Alan was the party's membership secretary. This was the beginning of a lifelong friendship. Alan became one of David's lightning rods that earthed him to the people of his future constituency.

David was a political novice in the 1960s but starry-eyed about the personality of Prime Minister Harold Wilson. Alan recalled his first lesson. 'David talked in percentages. I told him folk do not understand percentages.' A generation later a poll proved that 50 per cent of the population do not understand what 50 per cent is. It was a lesson that mathematician David took to heart. He matched his language to his audience. He spoke in vivid approximation of 'halves' and 'quarters' for mass audiences. Precision was the language for select committees and debates.

Alan was, and remains, in awe of one of David's rare talents:

> He never wrote anything down. On the doorstep he would get a dozen complaints, some of them were complicated. He never wrote details, names or addresses down. I don't know how he did it. He was just as good at remembering everyone's illnesses, children, business – everything. I've never met anyone like him.

Another lesson for David, the canvassing virgin, was the irrelevance of complex political facts on the doorstep. Alan's village is in Ibstock, a mile and a half from David's village of Heather. Their accents were identical. It was striking when I first spoke to Alan. His Leicestershire accent has distinctive clarity with soft cadences that were instantly familiar to me. The local accent is distinctively Midland and definitely not Brummie. Key phrases include: 'antenyonyergoranyonyer?' – 'Doesn't anyone have any?'; 'arse-ova-backuds' – 'I fell over' (quite badly); 'Ewayerdoublehewa' – 'He looked just like you'.

David became concerned that traditional English dialects and phrases were being wiped out by the all-consuming sound of voices from the south east. He blamed broadcasters for not allowing more regional accents on the airwaves. In 2007 he amended an Early Day Motion in Parliament, saying the phenomenon was part of the convergence towards the 'monochrome mush of effete estuarial English', to which he wanted to put an end. The character of his constituency was being disagreeably gentrified. He followed up his worry in a column:

'AYUP m'duck.' When I hear this, I'm either back in the constituency or it's one of the frequent occasions when I host a visit by constituents to look around the Palace of Westminster.

When I was a schoolboy attending Ashby Grammar, I was very aware of the different accents of my fellow students. Some came from communities in the Leicestershire coalfield like my home village of Heather while others were from villages just a mile or two away in the south Derbyshire coalfields such as Donisthorpe and Measham – who all spoke quite differently.

Sadly, both local accents and local words are in danger of dying out. Our rich local brogues are steadily being supplanted by anodyne and anonymous inflection-free voices, nowhere more so than in the broadcast media.

To his credit David never 'poshed up' his native speech patterns into received English. Many politicians have gone upmarket in the belief that local accents are political albatrosses. The speech rhythms and pronunciation of Alan Costello, the lifelong miner, and David Taylor, the MP, remained identical. Just as well, as Alan explained to David. 'On the doorstep round here, they are interested in only one thing. Are you from Ibstock or Heather?'

COUNCIL TURK

D avid's political baptism was a by-election for a
council seat in Ravenstone. It was a hopeless
battle. Labour had never won it. Alan Costello
explained his frustration:

> David insisted that everyone would receive a leaflet in
> spite of the fact I told him, 'These people will never
> vote for you. Why are you putting your head in a lion's
> den?' But he shocked us all. He won the seat. It was
> a narrow majority but he won it. For that to happen,
> hundreds of dyed-in-the wool Tories must have voted
> for him. It was the first example of the power of the
> Taylor Tories and David's broad appeal to voters.

On 30 June 1981, councillor Taylor took his seat for
the Ravenstone with Snibston ward of the North West
Leicestershire District Council. His impact was immediate. Lee Marlow, a reporter on the *Leicester Mercury*,
explained:

> At North West Leicestershire District Council I had to sit
> in the middle of the Chamber. There were three rows of
> Labour councillors and a smattering of Tory councillors.

I remember thinking 'Oh my God' – it was combat really. That's when I got to know David Taylor. He was the best councillor there. I remember one of the speeches he made against a Conservative councillor who had delivered a massive diatribe abusing single mothers in a local paper. David absolutely and literally ripped his argument to shreds in more ways than one. And it was impressive because it was passionate and it was eloquent. I remember watching open mouthed as he picked the article up, tore it into four pieces and threw it on the floor.

He was the best. I know that if anything ever happened to me and I needed help, even though he wasn't my councillor, I would go to him. I know there were people in other villages who didn't go to their own representative, they went to David.

From his first year as a public representative he was the councillor who would never say no to any constituent's pleas. David was a whirlwind who blew away the cobwebs of stultified council procedures. Prior to his appointment, the performance review role of the council had been largely restricted to investigating things that had gone wrong – sometimes apportioning blame and learning lessons so that mistakes were not repeated in the future. David had a different vision. He made a memorable speech likening the sub-committee's traditional role to the Spanish Inquisition and made it very clear that he had no intention of playing Torquemada.

He was the hyperactive, new broom chairman who galvanised the sleepy sub-committee into constructive action. First initiatives included a corporate plan; improved budget reporting with better supporting statistical and explanatory information; a restructuring of committee functions; improvements to member services; expansion of the use of direct labour and employment of apprentices. He pioneered the council's first equal-opportunities policy, which was adopted at the end of 1982. He also put measures in place to ensure that this policy was implemented and kept under periodic review. His fellow councillors gratefully accepted the leadership of the young resourceful member.

The 1980s were a time of angst and turmoil for North West Leicestershire. Disaster struck unexpectedly. Mining, the staple employer for generations, disappeared with the closure of seven pits and the loss of 10,000 jobs. David and his colleagues put measures in place to lead the district through the bad times. This included a local 'Plan for Jobs', covering capital spending plans, service delivery plans, employment plans, training plans and their resource implications.

Under David's guidance, the council sought practical, multiple ways to support and diversify the local economy, including allocating new sites for employment-orientated development; council house refurbishments and modernisations; full improvement grants for the local housing stock; a new council vehicle depot; a new leisure centre; reclamation of derelict land; establishment of a country park; and improvements to the public rights of way network.

David was one of five 'Young Turks' on the council

who shocked the senior members with their audacity. They were a little less ambitious than the Young Turks who campaigned against the absolute rule of the Ottoman Empire, but they were tough and determined. Under their pressure a committee was formed ostensibly to implement a Conservative government policy. Its real purpose was to filibuster and delay the implementation of the 1980 Housing Act that introduced Margaret Thatcher's sale of council houses to sitting tenants.

This was not mindless doctrinaire obstruction of council tenants' desire to have a fair deal. The council on which I served in the 1970s shared the view of the progressive smart socialists in North West Leicestershire. We recognised that long-term rent paying was theft. It was a financial cheat for those tenants who gave Labour their loyalty. The economic realities demanded that tenants should be allowed, even encouraged, to own an appreciating asset. Newport and Leicester councils had both been selling council houses for sound socialist reasons long before the Thatcher era. The work of Labour councils pragmatically giving the best deal to council tenants is largely disregarded in the myth that Thatcher was the first advocate of council home ownership by tenants.

But there was a profound difference between Conservative and Labour policies. David and his comrade Turks were adamantly opposed to the indiscriminate wholesale selling at massive discounts. Thatcher's law was compulsion that did not allow for local discretion. This provoked resentment. A group of five councillors devised an ingenious method for delaying the sell-off.

One of them, Canon David Jennings, told me that they set up a full-blown Housing Act 1980 Committee to sift applications. Its meetings were deliberately out of synchronisation with the main council meetings, which made the allocations unworkable by repeatedly ping-ponging them from committee to committee. The council officers were unhappy and the government department responsible decided that it was a ruse to frustrate the will of Thatcher's law. Jennings explained:

> David and I were sticking to our roots. Even though we had been selling some council houses for years, we loathed the compulsion in the 1980 Act. We set up a unique Housing Act 1980 Committee. Two years down the line we had not sold a single house. The committee took the applications, through solicitors and bounced them from one committee to another. The government jumped on us. We said we must be the only council in the country that has set up a special committee to deal with a piece of Tory legislation. It was a filibuster. Ultimately we had to comply with government demands.

The intelligent progressives alongside David Taylor included David Jennings, Mark Lupton, Bob Underwood and Vic Price. They were more adventurous and self-confident than their fellow senior councillors, some of whom had passed the peak of their powers. The whole Labour group shared the view that they did not want to tread water waiting for redemption from a new

Labour government. They wanted to provide immediate assistance to a local economy that was in meltdown.

The need to fill the gap left by the vanished pits was urgent and chronic. Their job was to attract new industry. They appointed one of the first industrial development officers in the UK and took the daring step of imposing full rates on empty industrial properties. This forced local landlords to cut rents in order to avoid losses.

It had a dynamic effect in attracting business and provoked one local landlord to offer a bribe to a councillor because the policy was hurting him. Again the council officers were nervous and jittery. They said the council was being used for party political ends. Officials always err on the side of caution. The Turks provided a fine example of practical bold decision-making that helped the area climb out of the doldrums of deepening unemployment. Council officers have their defined responsibilities. Elected councillors have higher duties to fulfil the political will of their electors.

One of David's best-remembered speeches in the council chamber concerned the constant delays to the local dream of reopening the Leicester to Burton railway line to passengers. The Ivanhoe Line – subsequently renamed the National Forest Line – was the missing transport link. David called it a mirage – as soon as you made a move towards it, it receded further into the distance. Sadly, this continued to be the case during his years as MP, in spite of David's ferocious and tireless lobbying.

During the bitter divisions of the 1985 miners' strike, the Leicestershire miners voted against the strike. The great majority of Labour Party members in the country disagreed. David found the situation difficult. He was queasy about Arthur Scargill's leadership, which he knew was driving the miners over the edge of a precipice. He believed that Scargill had imposed the strike decision on the union. Many others in the local party, including his close friend and keeper of the Labour Party flame Alan Costello, wholeheartedly supported the strike. Those who opposed Scargill were often crudely branded 'Right wing'. The labelling of politicians into largely meaningless Left and Right is the vernacular of the simple-minded. David was a serious politician with high intelligence and never an acolyte of any party sect. He adopted a principled position in this painful dispute, fully realising the harm it might do to his nascent political ambitions.

HUMBLE EXALTED

David's wife Pamela told me that David had no burning ambition to become an MP. He loved his family nest in Heather and he had found his métier as a councillor and a computer manager. Pressure from his day job forced him to withdraw from the council but his interest in politics continued. His party colleagues nudged him forward. Many politicians boast that they were 'invited' to stand for Parliament. This is a rare event in the Labour Party; aspirant MPs usually have to sharp-elbow their path into selection. Pamela said he 'drifted' into the candidature for the 1992 election. It was a tempting prospect. The prize was irresistible, the battle daunting.

The sitting Tory MP in David's constituency was distinguished only by the luck of sharing his name with the constituency market town of Ashby-de-la-Zouch: David Ashby. My memories of his parliamentary persona are clear. Parliament judged him to be an over-blown lightweight of little talent. Later he proved the accuracy of that opinion.

Had there been a prize for pomposity in 1993, David Ashby would have won it outright for his opposition to the Labour debate on sleaze in party funding. He said:

Let us have an end to all this mudslinging. Allegations have been raised about the Sultan of Brunei. We do not accept money from foreign governments or from families of foreign rulers. Those are the standards of this House.

Newly elected Labour MP Gordon Prentice intervened from a sedentary position, uncomfortably raising the spectre of a current Tory scandal, 'What about Michael Mates?' The former Northern Ireland minister had resigned earlier that year over his alleged links with the fugitive tycoon Asil Nadir. David Ashby revealed all the self-satisfied complacency of that era in his reply: 'The honourable gentleman is a newcomer to this House. I have been here for ten years and I can tell him that being an MP carries great dignity. Our word is our bond.'

On that deluded foundation a tottering empire of sleaze prospered. It took more than another decade to dislodge it. The expenses avalanche swept away both dishonourable and honourable MPs and buried forever the myth of blind trust in MPs' integrity. But the possibility of an expenses humiliation was an unforeseen terror in the early 1990s when David Ashby's insufferable pomposity was acceptable and not universally ridiculed as it should have been. MPs were bewitched by a blind faith in their probity and integrity as a rare honourable tribe.

The Labour Party nationally was optimistic of a Kinnock victory in 1992. Prime Minister John Major was floundering. In North West Leicestershire, David Ashby was not a charismatic figure; in fact he was widely unloved. A journalist described him to me as 'pompous ... a dreadful MP. He was difficult, always deliberately abrasive and prickly.' The North West Leicestershire Labour Party's expectations were high.

Labour had been ahead of the Tories in most of the national opinion polls since 1989. As 1992 dawned, the recession deepened. John Major hung on to office until the last moment. Labour were hot favourites to win the national vote; although the lead of the polls had changed from Labour to Tory on several occasions since the end of 1990, prospects for Kinnock were good when the election approached. The local constituency had firm ideas. Only a candidate deeply rooted in Leicestershire could unseat David Ashby who was bolstered by an inbuilt Conservative majority. David Taylor was strongly favoured as the Labour candidate but there were other local aspirant candidates. Bob Underwood was a respected well-known politician who had taken a far-left populist line. David Taylor had been the district council's vice-chair of the Finance Committee when Bob was chair. Revealingly and generously, Bob confessed his errors and warmly supported David in retrospect in an article in 2008:

> In truth, looking back I was a real nerd, with an outlook as blinkered as that of a horse whose vision was directed straight ahead by having to wear a hood in fear that it would meander across the track if allowed an

unrestricted view. I refused to participate in the annual Remembrance Day parade, challenging it as more aimed at glorifying the war than commemorating the fallen. What a prat! Hardly surprising that my attempts to secure the Labour Party's nomination as parliamentary candidate for North West Leicestershire (in 1992) failed. My friend and adversary was none other than David Taylor and it was he who beat off my challenge to take on the mantle of being the Member. At the time I was bitterly disappointed.

There was a powerful public response to David's candidacy. The party scented victory. David was convinced he was heading for Westminster. There were sound reasons for believing that a coup was in the offing. David had done it and had earned the reputation as a slayer of Tory dragons. It was his local roots, popularity and broad appeal that placed the deeply Tory ward on the North West Leicestershire District Council into socialist hands.

The intelligent resourceful campaign was masterminded by David and promoted by a loyal hardworking local party. He left nothing to chance locally but he had no influence on the opening national elephant trap. On polling day *The Sun* ran a front page showing the Labour leader's head in a light bulb. The headline urged 'the last person to leave Britain' to 'turn out the lights' if Labour won the election. This headline was widely regarded as the saviour of the Conservative government. The disastrous Sheffield conference was a further blow.

The voters were frightened off. They did not like Major much but they did not trust Neil Kinnock.

In North West Leicestershire, there was palpable evidence that the Tories who respected David were changing sides. The Taylor Tories became a recurring phenomenon at future polls. But the result was heart-breaking. David Taylor had wrecked Ashby's majority of 7,800 but tantalisingly fell short of victory by 979 votes. The national swing to Labour was a disappointing 2.2 per cent. But David's personality and record produced a swing of 6.0 per cent in his seat. The Labour vote was up by 9.7 per cent.

It was the worst possible result for the Labour candidate. A brilliantly successful campaign had avalanched votes to Labour but fell short of the victory that David had expected. He was deeply upset and was not stoical in hiding his feelings. 'I wept and David wept,' Alan Costello said. Others tell of the impossibility of disguising their emotions. Pamela says David was 'distraught'. David's daughter Jessica writes, 'I was always immensely proud of his achievements. It was heartbreaking to see him lose at the 1992 election by such a small margin. As a thirteen year old I was inconsolable after hearing the result at the count.'

Sharing the disappointment with his family was a hard blow. Years of fine work had produced little but the bitterness of failure. David Taylor, a fine aspirant MP lost out to an MP who was destined to bring ridicule and shame on the constituency.

DEFEAT AND ASHBY

Defeat is often fatal to candidates' aspirations. David's unexpected failure upset him deeply, but the close result stung and energised him. It was the spur for renewed ambition. The reluctant candidate metamorphosed into the dedicated passionate campaigner. How else could he compensate his family, and party, for their disappointment?

It is not a unique experience. I was cajoled into standing for a council seat in Newport in 1972. As a fully occupied father of two young children and a trade union shop steward I had no time to play councillors. I stood for the hopeless seat of Allt-yr-yn, which Labour had never won. I threw everything into the losing campaign. The inevitable defeat was life-changing. It left me smarting, hungry and eager for victory. That came two months later when I won a chance by-election, which led me to forty continuous happy years as an elected representative.

Fortunately I have never suffered the humbling gut-wrenching horror of losing an election when victory was expected. Pamela reports that David channelled his disappointment into a new determination to represent the area of his birthplace in Parliament. He had lost the first battle but he believed that victory in the ongoing war was to be his.

Labour veteran Tam Dalyell perceptively commented years later that David's defeat was a 'huge pity':

> Had Taylor won, he would have had five years in opposition and his sheer hard work and seriousness of purpose in asking sensible parliamentary questions would have won him a place in the ministerial team in 1997.

David never gave up his job at the start of the campaign. That would have been reckless. Instead he took unpaid leave of absence. He and his workmates were confident that he had left for good. Returning to the workforce defeated was a dispiriting anti-climax. This was the politics bad day. The premature pre-election expectations of his colleagues were well founded. The fall from the expected glory of Westminster back to the humdrum reality of his old haunts was a festering wound. He longed for the good day.

Many politicians never recover from election defeats. David used his narrow defeat as a springboard to recovery. The love and confidence of his family and the determination of the local party restored his hope. Needing a platform to pursue his campaign for 1997 victory, he was re-elected to North West Leicestershire District Council in December 1992. Again he successfully contested a by-election, this time for the Thringstone ward. It was a bold decision, akin to a football player failing in the top division and demoting himself to a lower division.

David was welcomed back to his first council meeting on 15 December when he was allocated seats on the Economic Development, Environment and Leisure Committees. By the May 1993 Annual Council Meeting, he was back on the more familiar ground of the Economic Development, Housing, and Policy and Resources Committees.

The winning Tory MP in David's constituency may soon have regretted his re-election. For the first time in his parliamentary career, David Ashby became a figure of national fame in a toe-curlingly embarrassing minor scandal.

He was accused of leaving his wife for a man after admitting spending New Year's Day in the same French hotel bed as a 'close' male friend. He denied having a homosexual relationship. He told reporters camped outside his family home that he was seeking legal advice over newspaper stories reporting claims by his wife, Silvana, that he had left her for a man. Meanwhile, the doctor linked to Mr Ashby in several newspaper reports issued proceedings for libel.

Britain was still living in the darkness of homophobia. The Ashby scandal was a titillating one for the coarse tastes of the media in 1993. Prime Minister John Major's conference speech lauded a return to basic values. The media perversely decided that he meant the virtues of chaste family life. The Ashby incident would hardly merit a paragraph in today's media, with our present indifference to unorthodox behaviour. Yet David Ashby was enslaved by his emotions not by his reason. He elevated an ephemeral minor scandal into a ridiculous career-wrecking calamity.

Mrs Ashby blamed Parliament's unsociable hours for the breakdown of their marriage. Speaking on BBC radio she refused to talk about her husband's relationships, but said: 'In Parliament many marriages are going wrong due to the terrible hours they have to work. It's a big destroyer of the family life ... Things can happen.'

David Ashby had issued a leaflet during the 1992 election campaign praising the merits of family life. The consolation of election victory was transitory. It was drowned in the nightmare embarrassment and hell of humiliation. Ashby told a court acting in his libel case that he had quarrelled with his wife every day for the previous six years and said she had often attacked him. Mrs Ashby claimed he had once tried to stab her to death. At one point during the proceedings, Ashby donned a grotesque mask with a hosepipe attached, which he said he usually wore to help him get to sleep. He claimed the unwieldiness of the contraption ruled out any homosexual acts while sharing a bed with other men! A judge said of Mr Ashby, '... he would in my judgment be quite prepared to tell a pack of lies if he believed it was just for him and in his interests to do so, in which case he could quite easily persuade himself of the truth and accuracy of an inaccurate account'.

Inevitably Ashby's judgement was found to be wanting. He lost the case. Penury was heaped on humiliation with a legal bill for the lost cause of £500,000. The *Sunday Times* twisted the knife in the wound. They described Ashby as a hypocrite for circulating a leaflet in the run-up to the 1992 general election saying he understood the needs of families. No one could claim that the picture of the Ashbys, which emerged during the trial, was that of normal family life.

Lesser politicians than David Taylor would have revelled in schadenfreude at the ignominy of their enemy. David did not. He remained silent. He knew the Ashbys. He was touched by the unhappiness of their being cruelly exposed to a mocking media and public. Most eager aspirant MPs would have been tempted to exploit this gaping weakness in the reputation of the sitting MP. The conventional advice would be that politics is warfare without any restraint expected or given. David broke the rules. His ideals were superior to the cruel weapons of coarse politics.

Labour leader John Smith told Prime Minister John Major that his 'Back to Basics' campaign was a hole that he had dug himself and then fallen into. David Ashby's reputation was savaged in Parliament. For four years David Taylor maintained his silence. When the opportunity for expressing a judgement came, he spoke with graceful generosity.

COMPASSIONATE TRIUMPH

The North West Leicestershire Tories deselected David Ashby. In the ruthless world of politics there is no room for compassionate understanding of human weaknesses. The crude warfare of election strategies doomed the chances of an MP who had brought the party and constituency into deep national disrepute.

David Taylor behaved with saintly restraint. He refused to play the game of coarse politics and join the witch-hunt of criticism and innuendo even though the constituency was the thirteenth most marginal Conservative seat in the country. David's Christian otherworldliness blinded him to the cruel realities of political combat. All parties would have deselected candidates in these circumstances. However unfair or inaccurate the criticism or allegations may be, the media myth becomes the accepted reality. Ashby was irretrievably damaged. He was unfit to defend a slender majority of 997 against a resurgent Labour Party and a supremely popular and confident local candidate of unsullied reputation.

New Labour leader Tony Blair was at the peak of his rave popularity. David Taylor was a certain beneficiary of the expected landslide. Once more the local constituency Tories helped. They chose Robert Goodwill as David's opponent. His previous and future political careers are characterised by Lilliputian achievements and serial election losses. He eventually won an election and became a member of the European Parliament. He unwisely expressed explosive and breathtakingly indiscreet views on expenses. *The Independent* reported him in 2000 saying:

> I fly from Leeds/Bradford to Brussels and we get a set fee of around £500, but if I buy a cheaper ticket, economy class for about £160 and £250, I can pocket the difference and, as a capitalist, also as a British Conservative, I see it as a challenge to buy cheap tickets and make some profit on the system.

In the 1980s I worked for an MEP. His conduct was above reproach but gossip indicated that the great majority of MEPs shared the flexible enterprising attitude to travel expenses described by Mr Goodwill. In 2005 Goodwill was elected to the Commons representing Scarborough. David Cameron sensibly exiled him to the silent world of the Whips' office. He has never overwhelmed the Chamber with his dominant presence. His parliamentary career appears to have peaked when he took part in an archery competition. The highest office he has held is secretary of the All Party Parliamentary Flag Group.

It was no surprise that Goodwill put up a feeble challenge to David in 1997. It was Labour's year of triumphant successes. The nation's anti-Tory revulsion and infatuation with New Labour's Tony Blair swept a record 419 Labour MPs into office. Goodwill was defeated by David Taylor's massive majority of 13,219 votes. David was entitled to his euphoria, buoyed up by 29,332 votes that was a heart-warming 57 per cent of the total vote. It dwarfed the Tory's 31 per cent share. All the Labour tears at the 1997 count in North West Leicestershire were ones of joy.

The constituency probably has a default position as a Tory seat. The North West Leicestershire constituency was created in 1983 from parts of the seats of Bosworth and Loughborough. It covers the same area as the North West Leicestershire district of the East Midlands and includes David's native square mile of Heather. It is divided between the main urban areas of traditionally working-class Coalville and middle-class Ashby-de-la-Zouch. The previous mining villages still clung to old Labour loyalties while the rural villages were Conservative inclined.

David recognised the message hidden in his splendid majority. The seat was a marginal one with shifting loyalties. He was never tempted to take his majority for granted. He braced himself for a parliamentary career of continuous campaigning to maintain a popular constituency profile.

MUFFLED FOOTFALLS

David savoured his victory as the first Labour MP for the seat. It made up for the bitter disappointment of 1992. His daughter Jessica tells of her delight at the triumph:

> I feel that my father's hard work was finally rewarded when he was elected in 1997. It was nerve-wracking to walk around the count but the sense of elation when he was declared the winner was amazing. That was the first election in which I was able to vote.

To those of us who hail from working-class backgrounds, the Palace of Westminster is alien territory, hostile and intimidating. Hung high on the walls are the smiling, stern or sneering portraits of royalty and aristocracy looking down on us in superior contempt at the influx of the peasants. In his book *In Place of Fear* former miner Aneurin Bevan said:

> The first thing a new working-class MP should bear in mind is that these were not his ancestors. His forebears had no part in the past, the accumulated dust of which now muffles his own footfalls. His forefathers were

tending sheep or ploughing the land, or serving the
statesmen whose names he sees written on the walls
around him, or whose portraits look down upon him
in the long corridors. It is not the past of his people
that extends in colourful pageantry before his eyes.
They were shut out from all this; were forbidden to take
part in the dramatic scenes depicted in these frescoes.
In him his people are there for the first time.

Nothing has changed much in the appearance of the
interior of the Palace of Westminster. It's getting worse.
In 2012, Parliament added an extra royal coat of arms
to the thousand royal mementoes already in the place.
The achievements of those who shaped our reformed
democracy – the Chartists, Tolpuddle Martyrs and
Suffragettes – are not recorded, except for one small
plaque in a cupboard. Without their sacrifices the fran-
chise would still be limited to rich males.

Although the walls are still bereft of socialist heroes,
when David arrived the corridors were crammed with
new Labour MPs. David was fortunate in discovering a welcome habitat in the camaraderie of 418 new
and senior comrades. He was already an experienced
politician armed with finely honed skills and powerful
principles. He was never 'New' Labour nor did he fit into
the Old Labour pattern of loyalties to the Holy Writ of
the 1945 Labour manifesto. He was a rare MP, being his
own thinking man. He judged all issues on their merits.

Among the vast horde of Labour MPs, there were
several groups that could not be disciplined. These

included the over fifty-fives who had no chance
of promotion because of ageism (Glenda Jackson
was the exception, armed with her ability plus two
Oscars); those who were enjoying their last parliament
as their careers drew to a natural close; those who
had experienced a freak 1997 result; those who intelligently judged that their chances of promotion were
nil because of ability deficiencies; those who believed
their personalities or abilities to be unacceptable to the
leadership for promotion; those who valued the causes
they espoused above patronage or personal aggrandise-
ment; and those who were later categorised by Tony
Wright as the 'Whys?' rather than the 'Whens?' The
'Whens?' are obsessed with when they will get promotion or favours. The 'Whys?' tirelessly question policies
and decisions.

David was a fifty-year-old able and eloquent 'Why?'
Embracing the New Labour nostrums would have
endeared him to the Blair leadership. David's rich background of achievements in local government plus his
native wit and ability would have ensured him an offer
of a ministerial career. But high office could have been a
prison that would have confined his soaring talents. He
was a new MP but also a seasoned politician.

The choice for all new MPs is complex. Either follow
the path of ambition and seek a ministerial role or
become a backbencher by choice. David judged that the
personal satisfaction of a minister's job would detract
from his ability to serve his constituents. Roaming as
a freebooter over all subjects would liberate him from

the strictures of blind adherence to all New Labour nostrums, both sound and foolish. He decided that his most constructive role would be as a friendly critic of the errors and excesses of Tony Blair.

Pamela told me that she and David often joked about the possibility of his becoming Chancellor of the Exchequer. 'It was never serious,' she told me 'but I know that he could have done the job and done it well.' David's first move as a parliamentary newcomer ruined any chance of promotion to a ministerial or shadow post. John McDonnell MP perceptively describes David's choice:

> On entering Parliament David took the career-destroying step of joining the Socialist Campaign Group of MPs and eventually became our Treasurer. He led for the group on monitoring and briefing us on the detail of some of the key financial measures put forward by the New Labour government. 'Socialist and proud of it' was his expression whenever asked why he joined the Group. Despite his background in accountancy and his detailed grasp of economics, he was a hopeless treasurer; largely because he was so nice he couldn't bring himself to cajole fellow Campaign Group members who hadn't stumped up with their subscriptions. As a result we discovered that he was paying many of our bills out of his own pocket.

The financial sacrifice he made by paying the dues of other members of the Campaign Group was not trivial. They were asked to contribute about £120 a year. The group was thriving in 1997 when Tony Benn was a regular attendee with thirty others. Topping up for tightwad members built up a 'debt' of thousands over David's twelve years in Parliament. His staff and family were later surprised by the scale of his secret generosity. His unselfishness was not news to them.

John McDonnell warmly praised David's abilities:

> He was a siren voice warning the government about the dangers of the demutualisation of the building societies, the deregulation of the finance sector, and New Labour's use of PFIs and so-called creative accountancy that all contributed to the credit crunch and the financial crisis. In any other era of a Labour government David would have played a key ministerial role and our country would have been all the better for it.

David had branded himself as friendly to but at a distance from Tony Blair's team. The government's loss was his constituency's gain. In his maiden speech he set out his bold ambitions. Proving John McDonnell's description of his kindness, his maiden speech began with a uniquely magnanimous tribute to his disgraced predecessor. The Commons convention is for all new MPs to thank their predecessors for their work. In the circumstances, David's tribute was of saintly generosity combined with a provocative attack on the press and the constituency Conservative Party:

> Let me begin by thanking my predecessor, Mr David

Ashby, who had represented North West Leicestershire as a Conservative since the seat was created in 1983. I first met Mr Ashby when we were opponents in 1992, and I found him then – as I have since – to be a courteous, thoughtful and industrious representative of our area. Let me express the appreciation of the 85,000 people of North West Leicestershire to David Ashby for his work over some fourteen years: we are most grateful for his unflagging efforts on our behalf.

Some people are due little in the way of thanks. David Ashby owes no thanks to the press, which hounded him unmercifully following allegations about his personal life. I deplore that. He has nothing for which to thank the courts, where he was the victim of an appalling legal decision when he tried to clear his name. I deplore that, too. His local association gave him few thanks when it deselected him because of the adverse media coverage. That was the most deplorable thing of all.

One of the first telephone calls that I received after the election was from David Ashby. He gave congratulations and much helpful advice about tackling the daunting role of a newly elected MP. That is the true measure of the man.

It was a model maiden speech, a *tour d'horizon* of the constituency's geography and key issues delivered with the assured authority and aplomb of an accomplished local politician comfortable with his own persona. Then, David had no fear that the devouring dragon of the press would one day torment him.

SUBSTANCE TRUMPS STYLE

It should not matter, yet the drab conformity of grey suit, blue shirt and red tie of male Labour politicians is an essential uniform. Our politicians' clothes should unobtrusively merge into the background and not distract from the verbal messages they broadcast. All politicians have experienced the irritation that ties or frocks get more attention in television interviews than the vital arguments that the politicians hope to convey to the nation. Originality in appearance, hair, make-up or clothes is not tolerated.

When Neil Kinnock dragged the Labour Party from its self-destructive militant ghetto of the early 1980s into electability, key MPs and candidates were 'Folleted'. Indifference to appearance was a chronic weakness that was a minor but sometimes crucial element in eroding candidates' appeal to voters. As a hopeful standard bearer for the party I was treated to sensible 'media training'. I was not important enough to be given the services of Barbara Follett, who carefully matched candidates' skin tones to colours that would add warmth and author-ity to their appearance. The process was helpful and knocked some of the rough edges off those of us who are carelessly untidy. The process never reached David.

David dressed with a similar individuality to that which characterised his political ideas and his imaginative doodles; to him every white space was a challenge demanding to be filled with elegant curves and geometric patterns. Externally he was an untidy mess that lacked grace. In his mind he lived in a world that revelled in a thrilling kaleidoscope of ideas, facts, fun, ambitions and ideals. His lifelong friend Canon David Jennings explained David's sartorial idiosyncrasies:

> He never dressed like most politicians. I think it showed a kind of casualness. It showed that presentation and image were not important to David. My wife says I'm bad; she says I'm scruffy and I don't care how I look. I don't know whether his family ever criticised David for that. Probably not. Vanity wasn't one of his weaknesses.

His daughter Jessica fondly recalls the exasperation she suffered. She knew that making David presentable for her wedding pictures was a Herculean task. Success could not last for a whole day:

> He had his own sense of 'style' and could not be persuaded to wear anything that he did not want to. If invited to black tie events he would simply turn up in a standard suit; he was not bothered about what people would think. When I got married I knew that I would not be able to get him into a morning suit but even getting him into a matching lounge suit was a challenge. He reluctantly came into the suit hire shop

with me and was the quietest and meekest I have ever seen him as he was being measured up. He does look good in the wedding photographs. As soon as he could, between the wedding breakfast and the evening reception, he changed into a suit of his own choosing.

One of his House of Commons staff, Daniel Crimes, pulled the veil back on a sartorial routine that was probably unique among the 650 MPs. He told me:

> David had a long-running battle with ties. All his ties were hanging knotted on the back of the door in his office. He would close his eyes and choose one and slip it on over his head! He was a man who took a total disinterest in clothes. I remember he had a pair of Converse One Star shoes, which he was secretly proud of because one of his daughters bought them for him. Quite fashionable. They had their own shelf in the Westminster office.

I once put our friendship at risk by demanding that he should come clean with me and confess that he was colour-blind. He was baffled. I came up with my clincher argument. 'The tie you are wearing is dark green, bright yellow and psychedelic blue. Your shirt is purple. That is not colour coordination that the rest of humankind would recognise. A female bird of paradise, possibly. But voters? Never!' He dismissed me as some kind of subversive taste fascist. Our friendship survived.

David had a wayward relationship with socks, which was not confined to his home in Heather. Daniel Crimes told me:

> There's a very sensitive subject about his socks. He would just dump them about the place in those green internal mailbags of which he was a keen collector. The only fashion statement he made was the colour red which he preferred for Westminster use. People always said he wore red socks. And he was rarely seen without his red scarf. I think he lost many, but they were quickly replaced. Red braces later became a must for him. Red was a political statement.

The *Leicester Mercury*'s Lee Marlow knew David well. 'David was acutely conscious of the need for publicity and went along with all our demands for unusual pictures. He jumped up in the air at East Midland Airport. During the campaign to save post offices, we persuaded him to be photographed sitting on top of a post box.' Perhaps the most contrived photo opportunity was a picture of David cutting a ribbon to mark the opening of, not a new building or a highway, but a lift in a residential home. 'The suit he habitually wore consisted of a jacket and three trousers,' Lee recalled. 'He said once that he was thinking of getting a second jacket. He would have looked scruffy in a morning suit.'

I once berated him because I failed to find the flattering picture of him that all other MPs used for election leaflets. I needed one to decorate supportive articles about his campaign that I had written on my blog. There were plenty of bleak pictures of him wearing his 'my kids have just bought another dog' face or dressed in his 'I've just come to fix the drains' clothes. But it was impossible. He was vanity deficient. I could not persuade him that a flattering authoritative persona would add gravitas to his pronouncements. Exposed braces and crimson socks were not the fashion accessories that media advisers encouraged to build an image of trust, admiration and respect.

Lee Marlow discovered a frustrated journalist in David. 'He devoured *The Observer* every Sunday and he'd say "Did you see that? Did you like the way he wrote that?" I remember once I said I quite liked Barbara Ellen and he said "Why on earth do you like Barbara Ellen?"'

David had a galaxy of newspapers in his constituency. I have one – the *South Wales Argus*. David had the *Leicester Mercury* (shared with other MPs) and exclusively the *Coalville Mail, Coalville Times, Ashby Echo, Ashby Times, NuNews, The Leader, Loughborough Echo* and the now-defunct *Coalville Echo* and *Ashby Trader and Echo*. To David, they were a great asset. They needed good copy to fill their pages. David abundantly supplied it. Lee said:

> I thought he had a really good way with words. He was a fiercely intelligent man but he wore that intelligence really lightly. To interview him as a journalist was good.

When I spoke to him one on one he was really clear.
He spoke in a really concise precise way. He wrote that
way as well and he was fond of word play. He wrote
regularly for the *Mercury*, the *Coalville* and *Ashby Times*
and also for the *Echo* – that's all three local papers. I
don't think he ever received any payment.

In addition to his 800-word columns, David contributed
copiously to the readers' letters pages. All his cuttings
were collected, labelled and filed for future reference.
He accumulated a good square yard of packed box files
stuffed with his news cuttings, epistles and photographs.
The newspapers gave him perfect conduits to inform,
amuse and woo his voters. The accurate portrait of the
model MP he represented was overwhelmingly persuasive. Opponents were disarmed and demoralised by the
total immersion of his constituents in endless reports
on David's beguiling honesty and exhausting diligence.

He wrote very well and not only about politics. It was
a very good deal for papers to have a highly readable
feature writer who described with charm and originality
his all-embracing interests. The Heather boy shared his
encyclopaedic knowledge of Leicester's monuments and
topography, its accent and patois, its wild landscape
and its havens of social intercourse. He celebrated the
skills of the local historians and drew on his lifetime
experience of seeing the transformation of his county
from mining communities to fashionable suburbs.

Knowing that readers are not attracted to great slabs
of writing, he often divided his contributions into

bite-sized lists. The most basic were the weekly diaries of his constituency work. They secured and cemented the trust he enjoyed from groups he visited. Other messages were conveyed in his beloved lists including Taylorised versions of the Twelve Days of Christmas, the Seven Deadly Sins, the Christmas Nine Carols and the Ten Commandments for MPs.

David understood that political writing is the least read of all journalists' work. Politicians frequently delude themselves into a belief that their turgid prose is read by newspaper readers who usually have the attention span of a caterpillar. Writing is not necessarily communicating. I once conducted a modest scientific study of how many people read political pamphlets. It was one in five. That's not the people who had them stuffed into their letterboxes. It's just one-fifth of those who were doing the stuffing. David deployed every journalistic trick to coax and seduce his constituents to read his outpourings. He was brilliantly successful in using enticing introductions that promised sensation, scandal or a fresh portentous truth. Lee Marlow is correct; David could have built a career as a fine journalist.

Strangely for a computer whizz he underachieved on the Internet. I frequently teased him about his absence in cyberspace. I was probably insufferably superior after setting up one of Parliament's first websites in 1998. It won awards because there were very few others competing with it. David set up his late in 2008 partly to silence my nagging. He was rightly cynical about some of the exaggerated claims made for the influence of the Web. He argued that it excluded many of his key constituents, especially the elderly. His site was simple and unambitious. I was unaware then of his prodigious output of words in his local press. I was baffled when he told me, holding his head in his hands, that he could not manage to write a fresh blog every day. 'Writing is hard work,' he said. 'How do you do it?' He also missed out as a member of the Twitterati. It's a shame. His serious ingenious persona and his gift for the *bon mot* never fully graced the Internet. He could have achieved star status.

BLOSSOMING INDEPENDENCE

Three months after his election David established his independence in a passionate defence of student grants: 'If we wanted to devise a system for emptying the universities of students and crushing talent in this country at an early age you could do no better than our present plans for higher education.'

As someone who had been robbed of the satisfaction of university life because of family circumstances he fretted over the tribulations of students and their parents:

> What sane, bright and motivated student would call the next three years of working flat out under endless pressure and living in poky expensive bed-sits anything like a life? And next year many of them will have to pay tuition fees too.
>
> Even today, while 80 per cent of the kids from the middle classes benefit from higher education, barely 20 per cent of children from working-class families go on to university. That's a social chasm we really have to bridge. If you think that education is the tax-payers' finest investment (as I do) in the future you might want an answer to one question. Why do we treat students

so badly? And why if the kids are from less well-off families do we really put the boot in?

So if you're in town on Saturday and see a down-at-heel character muttering to the world at large about having no money, show a little pity – their son or daughter has probably just won a place at university.

A *cri de coeur* from an anxious father.

David became so anaesthetised by lack of ministerial ambition that, comforted by his constituency popularity, he would indulge in some whimsical self-mockery. He developed an agreeable style of reporting on his exchanges with Tony Blair, with added local colour and idiosyncratic humour. He wrote in the *Leicester Mercury*:

Wed 21 July 1999, 4pm. Poky office in Old Scotland Yard.

Dear Tony,

You seemed very pre-occupied when I put my points about inequality to you in Prime Minister's Question Time earlier today. I imagine you are thinking a good deal about the coming reshuffle. I would like to throw my hat (the £9.99 bargain summer boater I bought at Ashby Show) into the ring as one who might be able to help you. Yes, we're talking about a Minister of Rural Affairs here. I've charged up my mobile phone and await your call.

Best wishes,
David

Mon 26 July 1999, 11pm. Kitchen, 10 Downing Street.
Takeaway enjoyably consumed.

Dear David,

Thank you for your letter. I was touched to find that
soaring ambition does not die at the age of fifty-two.

There is, I believe, a way ahead, but you must keep
it to yourself, or what I am about to say will have to be
withdrawn. I note that you are still a Parish Councillor
at Heather (wherever that is), perhaps because you
enjoy power of the sort backbenchers rarely encounter.
You have just the right background for what I have
in mind.

I am giving you a key strategic post responsible for
a micro-level analysis of a core rural concern. I want
you to become (the first ever in any western democracy)
Minister for Allotments. Unpaid, I'm afraid, as our
salaries budget is very stretched. Nevertheless, welcome
to government.

Yours ever,

Tony Blair

PS: Your handwriting reminds me of the importance of
David Blunkett's plan to extend our Literacy Hour to
include calligraphy!

David's commitment to his role and independence of
mind won him, by chance, a new fan in 2000. Veteran
MP and Father of the House Tam Dalyell discovered a
star. Years later he told me:

I vividly remember, on the evening of 17 February 2000, after a contentious vote on defence matters on a three-line Whip, lingering behind as the throng was emptying out of the Chamber for the adjournment debate, intending to leave when there was less pushing and shoving. Normally, adjournment debates are attended only by the MP raising the subject, the minister answering and a bored government Whip having to sit on the front bench. On this occasion I became hooked and didn't leave because Taylor was initiating a discussion on primary care of cancer patients, and it became clear to me that he knew a great deal about the subject.

What made me stay in the Chamber was the way that Taylor had obviously talked to the experts thoroughly and in depth. Over the years Taylor went on to be in the forefront of the campaign to make it government policy to have as a priority the early detection of cancer.

The central task for GPs has traditionally been to avoid overreaction to low-risk situations. Taylor was in favour of treating GPs fairly: if we expected them to refer more low-risk patients to specialists in the hope of detecting a limited number of early cancers, the taxpayers had to foot the bill. If, conversely, GPs were urged not to overload limited or expensive hospital facilities, we must not blame them too readily for missed cancers that could be a consequence of more restricted diagnostic strategies. It was characteristic of Taylor that he always saw two sides of an argument and that in matters of political policy there was no such thing, to use a phrase which was one of his favourites, as 'a free dinner'. He was a very realistic politician.

Tam recalled that the health minister at the time, Yvette Cooper, praised David for his choice of debate. 'As she put it, he really did contribute to the government's development of cancer services across the whole spectrum.'

Ambition or ministerial office still did not capture his interest. He never sought self-aggrandisement or empty publicity. His satisfaction came from worthwhile reforms. He spoke with sensitivity and understanding on the care of the elderly and the strains of family life. He inspired campaigns for improved residential care, the smoking ban and humane treatment of laboratory animals.

His range of interests was oceanic. He was double-hatted as a Labour and Co-operative Party MP and worked with prominent Newport Co-operative Party member David Smith on their shared passions. Well before Jamie Oliver they campaigned for free school meals as the most significant once-in-a-lifetime public health intervention to address health inequalities. Several pilot schemes resulted. Well aware that Harold Shipman, and other high-profile cases, brought a real loss of confidence in the regulatory system, he pressed for more lay involvement in regulating the NHS.

David took contemplative stock of the full impossibilist burden of the role he was creating for himself on his second Christmas in Parliament. In one of his columns, in seasonal style, he listed the demands of the job that were developing into a nightmare mission impossible:

On the twelfth day of recess my post-bag gave to me...

Twelve landfill lobbies... The numerous holes left by centuries of mineral workings mean that our area is permanently vulnerable to the attentions of the waste-disposal giants. The six short-listed Leicestershire sites for future decades are all in or close to this constituency. I am organising a national protest day in Parliament on 12 January to highlight the potential health risks of landfill sites – widespread support is promised.

Eleven local disputes... The second great commandment (love thy neighbour) can be the hardest to observe. Arguments across garden fences are as intense and durable as the ones across national borders which are their distant relatives. Hell is other people and our crowded island needs much better conciliation channels: but legal action is rarely the answer when Mark 12:31 is ignored.

Ten planning protests... Communities are better placed to fight off unacceptable developments nowadays, although most of the cards are still held by the landowners. I am often asked to involve myself in local campaigns and I do so if convinced of the cause and concern about the wider-scale impact of proposals. Parliament provides me with opportunities to work on improving planning legislation.

Nine dire decisions... The rapid growth of unaccountable quangos and impenetrable agencies in recent years has led to the Kafkaesque treatment of some people. MPs are often asked to give their support in complex disputes or appeals to higher authority. Only a minority are successful but it is crucial to assist wherever possible.

Eight mining matters... Most of this seat is still very much a coalfield community, though the last pit closed over six years ago. There have been several separate legacies from this – environmental (the lasting threat of open casting), economic (many replacement jobs are poorly paid) and social (the adverse health effects for former miners of decades in a very arduous job). Severe delays in paying compensation for work-related chest diseases are a current major cause of concern.

Seven social surveys... The number of pollsters who think the opinion of backbench MPs is important never fails to astonish me. They clearly don't share the media view that we are all mindless ciphers at the beck and call of our national spin-doctors. (Yes, I have had this comment cleared by the censors at our party's Millbank HQ!)

Six glossy leaflets... Why on earth do hundreds of organisations each month send MPs copies of their annual report, the latest in-house magazine, a product catalogue... My heart sinks when I think of all the trees crashing to forest floors to resource all this. Haven't any of them heard of the Internet for communication?

Five grants reduced... All sorts of individuals and organisations depend for their existence on grants of various kinds. When these are cut back, they contact my office for support and advice. And the lottery can only scratch the surface of that vast unmet need out there.

Four crushing blows... Like the lottery, Lady Luck does deal out her favours very unevenly. My office frequently hears of appalling hardships which people meet on the (often unfair) loss of a job, at the illness or death of a family member, or as the victim of a serious crime. We are a small part of a social-support mechanism (with the CAB, CVS and others) which tries to help pick up the pieces without adequate resources.

Three family homes... I only wish there were as many as that coming available every day. The embargo on local authorities using their sale proceeds to build more houses has at last been lifted. But the cash amounts involved are relatively small and will only ease the plight of a few numerous local people who contact me in desperation.

Two traffic demos... North West Leicestershire lies at the heart of the East Midlands transport network. Ministerial announcements in the last few months have left much-needed bypasses for Kegworth and Ashby in limbo. Campaign groups are quite rightly becoming agitated; the integrated transport strategy will work in the medium term. But, short-term, life in these two communities can be unpleasant and dangerous.

And a parent in poverty... Often because of a relationship breakdown and the subsequent involvement of the Child Support Agency. In its short (under-funded) life it has tended to catch sitting ducks in its net; only rarely the slow payers who have fled the nest and abandoned their responsibilities. The planned changes in legislation cannot come too soon for the many local families impoverished by the current system.

The challenges were grim. David was resourceful and tireless in taking them on. Ultimately the shadow between the shining dream and the drab reality was to become a burden.

CONSTRUCTIVE
EXASPERATION

A permanent dilemma for MPs is deciding how to organise their offices and staff to both serve constituents and fulfil the national and international role in Parliament.

Until 2002, all David's staff were employed in the constituency, doing the difficult tasks that David liked to do himself but could not find the time to do. There was sometimes an element of disappointment from staff who believed that working for an MP was an open sesame to the glamorous, power-charged, sparkling media-filled world of Westminster. The humdrum work in a drab constituency office can be a letdown. For four years I laboured happily for an MEP. So uncorrupted and hair shirt were we that in that time I never once visited Brussels or Strasbourg. But it was a very fruitful time for me. Politicians' staff who are reluctant to value the worth of the basic tasks in the constituency boiler room are doomed to brief spells of employment.

For a methodical man, David's methods for recruiting staff were casual and haphazard. Many were people that he had met socially; one had been placed next to him at a dinner party. He may have suffered the agonies of formally advertising vacancies and making choices. Working with an MP is a popular job. Almost everyone in the political world is convinced that they can do the work. Advertising a vacancy raises hope in a thousand breasts. Many apply. Only one will be chosen from scores of brilliantly qualified aspirants with immaculate CVs. The process is a torment and would have been acutely painful to a person with David's susceptible personality.

Bubbly, charismatic and brilliant, Lauren Otter worked for David for eight years cumulatively:

> I started very, very early on. I remember I was in Community Development and we invited him to an event we were doing. On the walk from the car park to the site I actually asked him for a job. A fortnight later he phoned me and asked 'Did you mean it, will you come and help out?' so I started helping out the following week.

That's it. No application or formal interview but the beginning of a long and fruitful working relationship. She continued:

> As an employer he was absolutely exasperating, but in the nicest possible way! He expected so much of himself, so he expected the same from staff. But he never complained if he didn't get it. He had such ambition. And he wasn't awfully clear on knowing when to

shrug and say 'Well you know, no one can ever be a
million per cent correct.' He didn't know when enough
was enough. Even with casework he always thought
there should be a perfect answer and detested saying
'Sorry, but we haven't succeeded on this one...'

Initially David had his staff working in temporary
offices in the constituency. In writing my books I have
had the effrontery to advise MPs: I sternly warned of
the hazards of a drop-in office in the constituency. In
my book *Commons Knowledge* I told the sad tale of one
Welsh MP's doom:

> He lost his seat because of the collapse of good rela-
> tions with his staff and the subsequent chaos of his
> constituency office. He set up an over-ambitious
> high street office, which became overwhelmed with
> constituents' drop-in queries. Staff could not cope
> with both callers and correspondence. Replies to letters
> were delayed for months. His diary became disorgan-
> ised and appointments were missed. A bad reputation
> for constituency work is as contagious as a good one.
> In spite of his good work in Parliament the MP was
> doomed to defeat.

My persuasive powers failed and David ploughed
on with his ambitious plans. In 2000 he moved into
a permanent Coalville base. My advice was wisely
spurned. Only a small minority of MPs have a fixed

base. Even fewer local parties own their premises. From August 1999 the local party agreed to raise money to purchase a site in Hotel Street in the town centre. It was previously a chartered surveyor's office. The local Labour Party members donated a massive £2,200 to help fund the venture.

A loan of £18,150 at zero interest was given to the area's constituency party, which allowed them to get a mortgage to buy the office and flat above. They intended to use the money generated from the flat to help fund the new office and ensure David was easily accessible to his constituents. David was already unreasonably accessible as compared to other MPs so he avoided the unwelcome media exposure that other MPs suffered.

Financially and politically it was a sound move. The 2001 general election was approaching and David wanted to shore up his reputation as a great constituency MP while creating a valuable property legacy for his local party.

Daniel Crimes was David's first employee at Westminster. He recalls:

David said that for the first three years of the first term 1997–2000, things were working smoothly in his office, exactly how he wanted them to. He had good procedures in place for responding and intervening as he wished. At that stage he hadn't quite developed his fiercely independent role. That came later after he had mastered the demands of constituency work.

Recalled with great sadness is David's long-serving caseworker Alison Harrop, who died of bowel cancer in 2007. David wrote with suppressed grief at Alison's death. His words reveal a great deal about David's character as well as Alison's strengths:

I am well aware, as a Member of Parliament, that I owe a huge debt of thanks to all those who help me survive what can be a hectic and exhausting lifestyle. One deserving such gratitude is my ultra-tolerant wife Pamela. Another is Alison Harrop, who sadly passed away two weeks ago.

I will miss Alison as a friend, as a political colleague and also as an employee. Since I was first elected back in 1997, she has been a pillar of strength in my constituency office where she worked as my casework manager, doing the detailed spadework to help solve the (quite literally) thousands of cases which people bring to their local MP in their search for help.

I consider myself very fortunate that Alison accepted the invitation to join my constituency team. Over the subsequent years, I saw time and time again at first hand the tact, talent, sensitivity and energy she deployed to handle the high volume of human problems which flow continually into our constituency office.

When she was diagnosed with cancer, she encouraged me in my campaign to get smoking in enclosed work and public places banned. Although she had given up smoking many years before, she believed that her earlier habit was the root cause of her condition. She fought bravely and stoically, endured both operations and treatments, but ultimately to no avail.

North West Leicestershire is a poorer and bleaker place without you, Alison. You'll be greatly missed. Goodbye and God bless.

BLESSED ASSURANCE

David's first Tory opponent to challenge for his seat was selected in May 2000. Nick Weston paid David the unavoidable compliment of tacitly admitting that the sitting MP was unassailable. The *Leicester Mercury* reported:

> The new Conservative parliamentary candidate has vowed to fight the party and not the man. It is hoped that Mr Weston's youth and passion will win the NW Leicestershire seat currently held by Labour's David Taylor. Mr Weston said, 'I am very excited about the new role which I face. I plan to campaign hard and really attack the opposition party's issues. I will not attack the man. I am hoping that a new bright future is on offer.

The cognoscenti will recognise the hollowness of Mr Weston's statement. The underlying message is: 'I have not got a hope in hell of winning against a popular MP with a 14,000 majority but I'll go through the motions anyway in the hope that I may be picked one day for a winnable seat.'

Meanwhile, in Parliament, David was learning new tricks. In June 2000 he took a vow of omertà. He had

promised to support a crucial new law – by not saying
a word!

Two MPs had announced their intention to amend the
Warm Homes and Energy Conservation Bill as it reached
its final stages. There was a possibility that, if the debate
lasted too long, the Bill would not complete its passage
through the Commons. David judged that silence would
give the best chance of success to the proposed new law
to end the scandal of people freezing in their homes. This
was a rare and unusual move for a professional talker.

The idiocy of parliamentary procedures that allows
destructive Bill assassins to destroy worthwhile reforms
sadly has yet to be reformed out of the system.

Two other issues were skilfully combined in a debate
that David called. There had been national publicity
about a raid at an animal trials laboratory at Harlan
on his patch. Though David had long been uneasy
about the ever-increasing rise in the number of trials on
defenceless sentient beings, he condemned the extremist
animal rights activists who used violent tactics against
the firm. He tried to steer a path through justified
concerns for animal welfare and the threat of violence
from protesters.

In the Commons he reported that staff at the centre
had been 'threatened, harassed and injured'. But he
also called on the government to raise welfare standards at such establishments. Throughout the debate he
wisely emphasised that he was directing his fire not at
Harlan but at all 300 breeding laboratories in the UK.
His conscience troubled him and he agonised about

his conflicting loyalties to constituents' jobs and the compassionate cause of animal welfare.

A stunt that called for muscle power not words was the annual parliamentary cycle ride to support Bike to Work Day. David joined the crocodile of other keen cycling legislators as they weaved their well-publicised way from the Department of Environment and Transport via Horse Guards Parade to Parliament. The next day he attended the grand opening of the 5,000-mile National Cycle Network which passes through major towns and cities and provides for journeys to work and school. It was a neat combination of serving his passion for cycling and making a powerful visual environmental point.

David and his team were relaxed before the election of June 2001. Tony Blair was enjoying an extended honeymoon of popularity, the polls were favourable and David had established himself as a brilliant constituency MP. The Tories were still waving a white flag in North West Leicestershire. In his election address, the Tory candidate Nick Weston said: 'This seat has been held not by Labour and Tony Blair, but by David Taylor. He has done a good job.' Realistic, but politically suicidal.

The Labour campaign was masterminded by David and his team from the new constituency office in Coalville. In his 'Parliamentary Patter' column in the *Echo*, David compared elections to end of term examinations:

In education, there are often stressful examinations to be taken at the end of each term, before you can move on to the next stage. Politics is similar, except for exams, read elections. And there are 70,000 examiners to be satisfied (or not)... As a parliamentary campaigner against noise, I feel guilty at adding to it. The public address system on my battle-bus sets off car-alarms, startles dogs, irritates some electors, but (I hope) encourages others to use their vote.

The expected victory agreeably followed national trends. The majority was down from 13,219 to 8,157 on a reduced turnout. No seats changed hands throughout Leicestershire. The press was bored by the result. They fretted about the non-issue of turnout even though the reduction in David's seat was less than the national average. The *Leicester Mercury* reported David's joining in concern about a turnout that was a respectable 66 per cent: 'I am relieved that we have held North West Leicestershire, but I am concerned about the reduction in turnout. There are worries there for all parties that we need to tackle.'

But generally he purred contentment:

This result sends out the message that people are happy with the way we are going in our economic policy and happy, in a broad sense, with our education policies. They remain unconvinced with our health service and want to see more in the fight against crime. However, they are prepared to allow us to continue in our work, both nationally and locally, and I thank them for their support.

The *Leicester Mercury* headlined their verdict, 'Personal vote takes Taylor through'. David and his party had earned their success and popularity in traditional Tory territory.

For once, cooing self-satisfaction was understood and justified.

FOR LOVE OF A MOTHER

David's blood was up when he sensed an injustice that demeaned his family's history.

He was immensely proud of his mother's heroic work in Heather. In May 2000, he returned to his childhood chore and volunteered to work behind the counter in Hugglescote post office for a morning. He said he wanted to hear why people do not want to see their post offices closed.

There had been a massive rally by postmasters and mistresses in London the previous month protesting against government plans to put all benefit agency payments directly into accounts from 2003. It was a dream campaign for David. He fought it at all levels of government. This was the moment he was pictured sitting on top of the postbox. He glowered, a threatening Buddha ready to ward off all interfering vandals who were out to bring down a beloved institution.

Worse was to come. In 2007, a new hit list of closures was announced including the one at Heather. This time it was personal. David now had a sharp individual imperative in the campaign. He pledged to fight the planned closure. 'I know from first-hand experience – and from visits I have made in the last few weeks to every post office in North West Leicestershire – that post offices are a vital part of the social fabric of our local community,' he declared.

David's family ran Heather post office and general store for several generations. The campaign followed the death of David's mother, Eileen, in 2003. She had been the dominant personality on the Taylor hearth and the main influence on the family's character.

When the great Jack Ashley died in 2012, his life-long friend Alf Morris recalled the influence of their mothers on their lives. Both were Labour MPs and heroic campaigners for the rights of the disabled and down-trodden. Jack was the son of a widow in Widnes, Lancashire. Alf Morris was also the son of a widow, in Manchester. Jack's father died when he was five, Alf's when he was seven. In his obituary Alf Morris said of his friend Jack Ashley:

> We were photocopies of each other, in terms of background. We also both wanted to change society. In Jack's case, and in my case, we did want to act and were determined that we would change the law to improve the status and well being of disabled people. Jack left the world a far better place than he found it. He was a family man and so admiring of his own mother, who was a widow in one of the poorest areas of the country.

Although David's mother was widowed when he was a young adult, David's political persona fits the splendid mould of Jack Ashley and Alf Morris. The presence of a dominant loving mother was probably the major influence in all three lives. Many other politicians have been influenced in the same way, including Neil Kinnock. Perhaps one day a study will be published on the powerful benign influence of strong mothers on shaping politicians with passionate ideals.

Alas the fervour, guile and enthusiasm that David put into the fight to save Heather post office were not rewarded in victory. The Post Office announced:

> Respondents' main concerns were the availability of public transport, the impact of a closure on elderly customers and concerns for the future of the adjoining shop, which is the only one in the village.
>
> There are low customer numbers at Heather branch and there is evidence of high car ownership locally. The main alternative branch at Ibstock is approximately 1.5 miles away and has free car parking available. The second alternative branch at Ravenstone is just over two miles away and is served by a regular bus service which has a concessionary scheme for elderly and disabled customers.
>
> Taking these and all other relevant factors into account, Post Office Ltd has decided to proceed with the closure of Heather branch.

It is difficult to disagree with the cold logic of the verdict's officialese. To David it was a personal rebuff, a breach in continuity that diminished the inherited worth of the work of his family in serving the people with a vital post office and general store. His opposition was visceral. The years of sacrifice by his mother, the endless grind without days off or holidays, now ended in empty nothingness, leaving only a thin legacy of regrets and proud memories.

MASTER INTERROGATOR

David Taylor was a supremely resourceful questioner. Former Father of the House Tam Dalyell told me that David meticulously 'sculpted' his questions. About half of MPs' oral questions can be prepared well in advance. The others are opportunistic and sometimes impromptu. Until the arrival of Speaker Bercow, rambling long-winded questions that had not been properly prepared were tolerated. Question times were usually tedious as members aimlessly babbled. The senior, excessively confident, members were the worst offenders. They were so relaxed they made it all up when they were on their feet. A small minority of MPs are brilliant impromptu inquisitors. The majority dribbled verbal ectoplasm laced with Polyfilla clichés and platitudes.

Speaker Bercow has now set new standards by harrying the long-winded time gluttons. David had been the exemplar of good practice for many years. The Chamber eagerly anticipated his oral questions. They were always word perfect, pointed and significant. His challenges to government ministers were usually in the tail of his questions. Frequently they began with shameless flattery of the answering minister. His intention was to disarm before the barbed query struck.

The praise was never overstated; just enough to convince the recipient of the compliment that it was based on the truth. Examples include: 'I know the honourable gentleman well from our days on the Environment, Food and Rural Affairs Committee and respect him greatly', 'I exculpate the minister, who is a very able man of great integrity...' and 'the Secretary of State is known for not being swayed by passion, and for being an open-minded man who is happy to rely on science and his advisers'.

Ministers were grateful, distracted and receptive. It was difficult for them to do anything but answer David's kindness with cooperative conciliatory answers. Shades of the Court of King Canute survive on the banks of the Thames.

The House of Commons library kindly measured for me the extent to which David mastered oral questions, including the newly fangled topical ones. They produced tables of the total questions asked by all 650 MPs. David tops them all with a massive eighty-four topical questions and 121 other orals in the year 2009. Many were opportunistic, called because of his permanent presence in the Chamber.

David's intention was to pack a substantial fresh message into fifty to eighty words, expressed in jargon-free newly minted original sound bites. The final words usually posed an unanswerable penetrating question that left the minister floundering with a response that

Above David with his older sister Margaret.

Left Held aloft by his mother Eileen, David, aged two.

Above David, his older sister Margaret and his younger sister Susan shared an idyllic childhood.

Left From his early years, it was obvious to all that David was exceptionally intelligent.

Below After the death of her husband, David's mother Eileen (right) became the village post lady, alongside another, Edna.

Above With an intense pride in his family, David devoted himself to his wife, children and grandchildren.

Below Daughters Jessica, Sarah, Catherine, Rachel and granddaughter Naomi.

Above left An enthusiastic cyclist, David always had wife Pamela by his side to provide moral support.

Above right David and Pamela in Romans-sur-Isère – Coalville's twin town in France – August 2007.

Below Riding the Pennine Cycleway with pal David Bennett.

Above A visit to Hall Lane Methodist Church Pre-School in Whitwick, 2001.

Right David in a lighter moment.

Above During the state opening of Parliament, David would always appear in full view of his admiring constituents, in among the party leaders and prominent frontbenchers. How did he do it? Sharp elbows!

Below Coronet Copse, near David's home village of Heather, is renamed David Taylor Wood. His grandchildren Henry and Naomi 'unscarf' the handsome new sign.

On Boxing Day 2009, David Taylor died of a heart attack. *Above* The welcome new practice of applauding the dead was an eloquent expression of the warm regard the people of North West Leicestershire had for their MP. *Below* David's wife Pamela and four daughters lead the procession to David's private burial.

David Taylor 1946–2009.

was inadequate in substance and language. The range of his interests was mountainous.

His vocabulary, grammar and aphorisms were testaments to the quality of his education in Ashby Boys' Grammar School as he frequently reminded us. In an article in 2009 he said:

> that early grounding in the English language was drilled into me so much that I am now a person who gets annoyed by incorrect use of the apostrophe and the split infinitive, while despairing of the nu-language of texting. My personal pet hates include many examples of modern day lingo and clichés. How on earth can you love someone 'to bits'? Can something really be 'infinitely better'? Or '(the late so-and-so) didn't deserve to die like that' – so just how did they deserve to die? And don't get me going about 'for free'!

Not many MPs habitually use words such as 'egregious', 'exculpate', 'chutzpah', 'eviscerate' or 'excoriate'. They brightened parliamentary discourse and shone like jewels among the prosaic dross of Whips' written hand-me-down questions that pedestrian MPs use.

At their best, oral questions are concentrated mini speeches reduced to their potent essence. Many are masterpieces of the politician's craft. No word is redundant. Every adjective has been carefully selected and weighed. The barb in the final words is sharpened, poison-tipped and often splayed into three points: 'prohibitive in cost, flawed in concept and intolerable in consequence?' or 'exorbitantly expensive, utterly unreliable and lamentably late?' The hapless answering ministers usually floundered attempting to answer one point. Three were impossible.

David confessed that his addiction to alliteration should be curbed. He never managed to do it. Sometimes the weight of the consonantal ballast buried the message.

Will you say what protections, for instance, the Manchester City supporters have against the attentions of the unsavoury Thaksin Shinawatra or is it forever the fate of football fans to be fleeced by flaky foreign financiers?

It is a full twenty weeks since the publication of the Green Paper and the start of the present campaign on attendance allowance and disability living allowance, so will the honourable gentleman confirm the rumour that the leader of his party will sack the head of the section for opportunism and scaremongering in Tory Party headquarters for tardiness and incompetence?

Will the minister press the government office for the East Midlands to respond to my urgent request for a call-in? Because to describe the present position as a dog's breakfast would be a grossly unfair slur on canine eating habits.

The government's plans provide further proof that the inverse care law is alive and well. As the minister will know, the idea was first proposed by Julian Tudor Hart in 1971. His law states that the availability of good medical care tends to vary inversely to the need for it in the population that it serves. Put simply, those who need health care services the least use them more, and more effectively, than those with the most need.

The EU estimates its costs to the UK at £15 per person a year, while the Europhobic *Daily Express* assesses it as £250 per family a year and the Taxpayers' Alliance – the Tory Party agitators of the honourable Member for Shipley (Philip Davies) – put it at an astonishing £2,000 per person a year. Which of these figures remotely resembles the truth?

Has there been any indication from the Chancellor of the Exchequer that he intends to confirm in a statement that non-domicile tax status will not apply to rich kids living in Richmond and Kingston unless and until those two boroughs secede from the United Kingdom?

Does the Solicitor-General believe that the proposed Bribery Bill would deal with the Leader of the Opposition's promise to make amendments to the inheritance tax regime which will benefit only the people on his Christmas card list?

Having five years ago been given exclusive rights to dip its corporate snout into the private finance initiative hospital trough, Laing O'Rourke must have industrial-strength chutzpah now to sue the Secretary of State for Health for abortive costs on that collapsed project. Does that not lay to rest, once and for all, the illusion that PFI transfers risk to the private sector?

The original hope was that the A400M would replace the C-130 and C-160 aircraft, and its initial brief was to operate in many configurations, including cargo transport, troop transport, medevac, aerial refuelling and electronic surveillance. As the German government intend to pull out of the consortium because of cost and delivery overruns, how does the Secretary of State respond to the charge that this programme has become a show horse for experimental new technologies, which has led to it being exorbitantly expensive, utterly unreliable and lamentably late?

Last week's National Audit Office report on C-NOMIS excoriated senior NOMS management for an information and communications technology project whose lifetime costs have tripled to £700 million in just three years. I exculpate the minister, who is a very able man of great integrity, but what should be done about the lamentable failures of that ill-conceived, incoherent and incompetent organisation? Perhaps the guilty parties in EDS, Syscon and NOMS could be locked up for

egregious negligence as a pilot group in one of the minister's fabled titan prisons – if there is one big enough.

More than 10 million people in the English midlands
have a similar socio-economic and demographic profile
to that of the people of Wales. They look over Offa's
dyke with some envy at the public expenditure that is
possible through the Barnett formula. Will my right
honourable friend see me to ascertain how we in the
English midlands can get such support? Is he willing
for us to have honorary status in Wales as Powys, East?

The Secretary of State is known for not being swayed by
passion, and for being an open-minded man who is happy
to rely on science and his advisers. The Environment
Agency has said that the third Heathrow runway would
exceed EU pollution limits because of unsafe nitrogen
dioxide levels. How would it be right for such advice to
be discarded in a cavalier and cursory fashion?

I believe that Sir Peter Tapsell went wrong in saying
that the benefits provided to those who might be
squeezed out of work would be infinitely more generous than they had been. That gives the impression that
people can fall back on cushioned indolence. That is
the impression held by some members of the journalistic profession. It is not the case, however; benefits
are a base from which to work, but they are certainly
not generous.

Does the Home Secretary not find this situation rather ironic? Here we are, on almost exactly the twenty-third anniversary of the climax of the Westland affair, when the Tory Secretary of State for Trade and Industry was leaking furiously against the Secretary of State for Defence. Is she as unsurprised as I am that a party that had more leaks than a Rhondda vegetable show when it was in government should be actively soliciting leaks when it is in opposition, in the disgraceful way that we have seen over recent months?

Is it not the case that the NAO has a target of saving the taxpayer £9 for every pound that its operations cost? Would the NAO not be able to do that much more easily if it had a proper grip on the £250,000 million-worth of private finance initiative projects, which are prohibitive in cost, flawed in concept and intolerable in consequence?

The delayed agreement and sign-off of defence information infrastructure stage 3 is but the latest debacle for a benighted project that has already more than tripled in cost to more than £7 billion. Why are civil servants and politicians so obsessed with outsourcing public sector IT contracts, given that the logic and economics of extra costs and complexity point in precisely the opposite direction?

Last time I looked, the objectives of the Audit Commission were to drive efficiency and effectiveness in local public services, but last week its chief executive dismissed critics of public sector cuts as 'shroud wavers'. Will the minister have a quiet word with Mr Bundred, put him back in his box and explain that one of the roles of the public sector is to help to sustain the economy during a time of recession?

I know the honourable gentleman well from our days on a Select Committee and respect him greatly. He criticises our promotion of matters European, but does he not think that the group that his party has joined in Europe is the most extraordinary mix of oddballs, malcontents, misfits, flat-earthers and unregenerate nationalist bigots? Is that not a fair and even-tempered description?

The centenary year of Girl Guiding UK has just commenced. May we have a short debate on the merits of that estimable organisation? It has 100,000 adult volunteer leaders and 20,000 supporters providing a framework that enables 450,000 Rainbows, Brownies and Guides to enjoy a girl-led programme that builds skills, confidence and self-esteem in a phenomenal way.

David was not just the most skilled questioner; he freely passed on his advice to other members. Scottish MP John Robertson was as bewildered as any other new MP when he first arrived. John was elected with little preparation at a by-election in 2000 following the unexpected death of Donald Dewar. By-election winners are lonely vulnerable figures braving the mysteries of the House without the camaraderie of fellow freshly elected MPs.

John noticed that David was ever-present, ever-talking, ever-questioning in the Chamber. He sought advice from David on making a good impression. John recalls the advice was to pick half a dozen subjects that interested him and work them into the questions of the day. Often they would not be relevant. With a bit of practice, vital extraneous matter can be dragged into almost any question as long as some words of genuflexion are included to give a spurious link with the content of the original question called.

David may have quoted one celebrated example of Tony Banks. Tony was desperate to raise the subject of Norway's decision to renew whaling. He stood seeking to be called on a dozen subjects at Foreign Affairs questions. His tortuous links were not put to the test until Speaker Boothroyd called him on a question on the export of bananas to the West Indies. Tony said, 'The people of Norway are going bananas about the killing of whales...' Speaker Boothroyd allowed the question because she admired the chutzpah.

Part of David Taylor's benevolent persona was to play the role of Chaucer's ideal mentor, 'Sownynge in moral vertu was his speche, And gladly wolde he lerne and gladly teche.'

CLOCKWINDER

David's Christianity was not superficial or sprayed on. It was far from the silent acquiescence of limp-faithed or agnostic politicians who do not want to antagonise their constituent believers. There are few straightforward decisions in politics. David frequently had difficult paths to tread between conviction, loyalty and political expediency.

Canon David Jennings explained:

> His Christianity went deep, but it never came up as an obvious thing. He served as a churchwarden, a very significant office. Technically the churchwarden is the Bishop's representative in the parish. He is responsible for seeing that the parish priest fulfils his or her duties and that the fabric and the building and the ornaments of the church are properly looked after and cared for, and to report to the Bishop if there are any problems or difficulties. Churchwardens have the power of arrest in the church if somebody is misbehaving.

When he was first elected David was tempted to abandon his onerous church duties. Canon Jennings urged him to continue. 'I said to him, don't give up being a churchwarden. It's actually saying something very important about who you are.'

He remained in the role for a few years but he found the workload of diocesan meetings impossible. But he continued to wind the clock in the church tower at Heather. It was not just a weekly task; he had to climb the village tower twice a year to stop or advance the clock hands by sixty minutes.

David described himself as a committed Christian and an ecumenical Anglican:

> My Christian faith gives me a personal moral compass to help map out both private and public life. It's a faith I learned about at home. Christianity was a really important part of our household. As children we were encouraged by our parents to be part of the life of our church – Sunday school, choir, church council.

David's views could have put him in conflict with his progressive left-wing friends in Parliament. Few of his fellow members of the Campaign Group would agree with him on abortion and euthanasia. Both issues troubled him. One friend repeated the canard that his views on abortion were influenced by the loss of his premature son a few hours after birth. That is unlikely. On moral issues his head ruled.

He rejected the call for more autonomy in end-of-life decisions that are championed by the great majority of MPs. His Westminster staff disagreed with him. One of them told me:

He was focused on abortion and his attitude hardened over the years, especially on the unborn and preservation of life. I didn't particularly agree with him on those issues, but I respected him. They were his religious beliefs. He had a view on euthanasia and would have rock solid support from the hospice sector but not from his friends.

These two thorny issues were never the cause of dispute at the Peter Pike table in the Members' Dining Room. The nine-seater table was still known by the name of the Burnley MP in the 2005–10 parliament, even though Peter did not contest the 2005 election. He had been an MP since 1983 and he ate there among his independently minded friends almost every evening of his long parliamentary life. David Taylor was a regular, as was I. We had shared convictions on most subjects. Unlike David, most of us were fully paid-up humanists and agnostics. The other regulars included Gordon Prentice, Kelvin Hopkins, Lynne Jones, Geraldine Smith, Lindsay Hoyle, Ann Cryer, Bob Laxton and me.

By parliamentary standards the meals were generally simple with a modest amount of alcohol. No one was ever drunk, or even worse for wear. Conversation and comradeship was our bracing champagne. Only David, Kelvin and Lynne were members of the left-wing Campaign Group. Other dominant members of that group – Dennis Skinner, Ronnie Campbell, John McDonnell – never set foot in the Members' Dining Room. They were the hair-shirt wing of the Campaign

Group: the Sybarite wing allowed themselves the occasional dip into modest chaste luxury. Alan Simpson, the godfather of the group, arranged a meal for the members in a Harry Ramsden's fish and chip shop at a party conference. That would have been basic in the midst of routinely sinful conference excess. Dennis Skinner refused to come because he did not want anyone to serve him food.

The Peter Pike table group was liberated, creative, resourceful, funny and devoted to the values of classic Labour. David Taylor was the unquestioned leader on practical opposition to the financial sins of New Labour. Gordon Prentice was the valiant persecutor of Lord Ashcroft and top Witchfinder General in pursuit of Tory wickedness. Lynne Jones was the erudite fearless seeker after solutions to social security and educational dilemmas. Kelvin was the voice of trade unionism blessed with an elephantine memory for political history and a superb knowledge of the quality of wines. He was a proclaimed 'expenses angel' who combined tiny expenses with a '*bon viveur*' tendency. Geraldine Smith was attuned to the voters' mood as the repetitive victor of the 'unwinnable' Morecambe seat. Lindsay Hoyle was grass roots Labour by lineage and conviction. Ann Cryer was the fearless, principled scourge of the self serving. She took on male Asian prejudice by attacking forced marriages and exposing the consequences of consanguinity. Possibly uniquely, her first husband and her son were also MPs. We refreshed and invigorated each other's ideas and spirits. That camaraderie was a high point of my twenty-five years in Parliament. The 2010 election scattered the

regulars mostly outside of the House. The solidarity of
the Peter Pike table is no more.

Matt Mulley spoke of the occasional dislocation
between David's socialism and his Christianity. Matt
had two part-time jobs, one with David, the other with
New Labour über-loyalist Anne McGuire. He told me:

> Although they disagreed on many things their faith influ-
> enced their politics. On points you would often think they
> would disagree on, their faiths brought them together on
> abortion, stem-cell research and end-of-life care.
>
> David was a very faithful man. If he pinned his
> colours to something he would stick with it. If his faith
> decreed that something was wrong, he would follow his
> principles. On abortion, he never spoke to me about
> losing his son. His stance on this issue was simply from
> faith. He always walked in a straight line from where he
> was to where he wanted to be. If the politics were ever
> an issue and made a hill or a valley he would just walk
> straight through. He was very single-minded. He felt if
> he was true to anything other than his principles, there
> would be nothing left.

David found no difficulty in expressing his faith simply
and sincerely to his constituents. In his Christmas
message in the year 2000, he wrote in one of his newspaper columns:

> The Christmas period is even more special this year, for
> we are commemorating the 2000th birth of one whose

message has been unchanged throughout those twenty centuries of change which separate his time from our own. It is to love thy neighbour as thyself. That is as concise a definition of community spirit as I have heard.

Canon Jennings said:

He was one of those sorts of people that I just love. Because there's no side to them. They're down to earth with significant values, with considerable integrity and actually live what they believe. Now, how many people really do that? I think one of the biggest problems in society is a kind of individualised personalised schizophrenia, where people admit or suggest they hold certain values but their lifestyle doesn't match those. David was a holistic person. That is, he lived his values. And you don't see many of those sorts of people here. And I expect you don't see many of them in the House of Commons either.

No. Except at the Peter Pike table.

FAMILY JOY

David glowed with pride in his role as a father. He valued his own family inheritance and was determined to pass on his parents' high standards to his children. His third daughter Jessica reports:

> He always wanted us to do the best we could. Sometimes the standards he set and the expectations he had would seem very high. He was proud of what we achieved; he just did not want us to waste our talents and intelligence. We did not simply receive pocket money when we were young; it had to be earned by answering mathematical questions such as multiplications, or by washing cars.

Daughter Sarah remembers a time when David's legendary mathematical calculations went awry:

> Dad awarded us a set of financial incentives for each particular grade we achieved at GCSE/A level/Degree. An 'A' was £x, a 'B' was £x etc. However, he quickly reviewed these criteria after the first of us, Rachel, received her results. To honour his pledge Dad would have had to buy her a small car to reward her for her set of GCSE results. The value of the incentives was then drastically scaled back.

David always gave the best of himself in nurturing his family. Jessica recalls that she would sometimes ask David for help with university essays:

> On one particular occasion I had an essay to write on the reasons for and the impact of the minimum wage. I rang him to ask for some information and had to confess that the essay was due in the next day. He was annoyed with me for the lack of notice but he duly rang me back a short while later with the necessary informa-tion. *We* got quite a good mark for that essay.

He was a devoted and inventive dad who always had time to help his children. 'I would often spend the night before an assignment was due either discussing his feedback over the phone and quickly making the amendments, or up until the early hours working on the computer with him on it,' Sarah recalled.

Jessica remembers the ingenuity of her father at making special occasions memorable. Though birthday cards themselves were well received, it was the artwork on the envelope that had the most impact. David, not an artist himself, would cover the envelope with doodles and decorative writing.

Family birthdays are also fondly remembered by Sarah:

> When we had birthday parties as children Dad would always arrive part way through (after getting home from work), normally while we were on the jelly and ice-cream course. His favourite activity was to wind us

all up by asking us to repeat after him, 'ice scream/I scream, arrrrgh', 'you scream', to which the response from a group of young girls was 'arrrrgh'. Then he would add, 'we all scream together', to which the whole house erupted into a screaming contest. Dad would then use his arms, like a conductor in an orchestra, and raise and lower his hands to raise and lower the tone of the screaming! Mum, as you could imagine, would probably be ready for a sit down during this part of the party, but there was no let up once the screaming orchestra competition started.

Family life in the Taylor home sometimes revolved around the great socks searches. Jessica told me:

Dad was always buying socks. If he could not find a pair of socks (i.e. if someone had not paired them up for him) he would go out and buy a few new pairs of socks. Socks were of various shades of red and black which made them hard to pair up. Mum would then hide the new socks away as there was already a basket full of unpaired socks. She therefore had a stash of new socks which she would let him have once he had got rid of the old ones.

The four daughters of Pamela and David have been blessed with great ability. They have all been diligent successful students. The devoted father had a cunning device to ensure all his daughters felt equally loved. Jessica reports:

He never declared any of the girls to be a favourite and had a running joke of FDx (Favourite Daughter number?) which applied to all four of us. He enjoyed it when we were able to visit him at Westminster. He would be able to be a tour guide and pass on lots of interesting facts. His ability to absorb and retain information astounded me.

I have inherited his mathematical brain and have followed him into the accountancy profession. I think that he was pleased about this and was proud of my achievements. His mental arithmetic always far surpassed mine – I always find myself reaching for the calculator. I would send him my ACCA examination results by text, which he stored on his mobile. I told him one set of results verbally and he asked me to send them by text too so that he could have the complete set saved on his mobile.

When he was at home and had a few minutes to spare he would ring each of us up just to check that we were well, or he would simply send a text saying 'RUOK?' He always passed on articles or papers he thought we might be interested in. For me, it was accountancy or tax-related articles.

Throughout David's parliamentary career Pamela was protective of the privacy of family life. While there are some advantages to being the children of politicians, they can be exposed to the catcalls and ridicule of school life where politics is coarse and brutal. I confess that I strove to protect my children and stepchildren from the dropout from tabloid hysteria. The most hostile response I had from any vote was when I voted against 92-day detention without trial. The tabloids listed and denounced all the Labour MPs, including David, who voted against this illiberal counterproductive stunt as 'friends of terrorism'. Politicians grow hardbacks to protect them from abuse. Children do not. The courage of all independently minded MPs could be dented by fear that the price of their courage could be the school-yard bullying of their children.

Pamela understood the wounds of politics that her husband suffered. Sometimes the insults and the abuse could be challenged and diminished. Other blows damaged at a deep level. Few, outside of the parliamentary family, understand the hell of despair suffered by genu-inely honourable members over the expenses scandal. No MP had a notion of the torment that lay in wait for us.

In my friendship with David, I understood a little of his intense pride in his family. He drew his strength from them. It was close to the ideal family life. Pamela and David shared the same values in a partnership of love, loyalty and respect.

A charming memento of the inevitable strains and irri-tations of family life is this agreement that David drafted when a decision on a new family pet had to be made:

28/3/91

We the undersigned, being members of the Taylor Household, do recognise that the acquisition of yet another dog goes right against the wishes of David

Taylor and also breaks a commitment given that the previous animal obtained would be the 'last one'.

We also recognise that, in the view of David Taylor, our home in recent times has: smelt of animals and unemptied cat litter trays; been a disgraceful tip (especially the bedrooms, dining room, lounge and kitchen); had a lawn strewn with straw, hutches and other rubbish and a garage littered with straw; had breakdowns in domestic arrangements, particularly in relation to washing of clothes and pots, taking of telephone messages and general unwillingness to help by younger members.

In forcing yet another animal on David Taylor we do agree that in future we will: eliminate all animal smells, empty litter trays daily and clear up their mess; each tidy up our own rooms at least weekly and share the job of cleaning up other rooms willingly; undertake our share of animal care on an agreed rota (when asked); keep the garden clear of animal-related rubbish (when asked); keep the garage free of straw; do our share to make the household run a lot more smoothly than it has done lately.

If these agreements are not upheld, we accept any consequences that may arise which in the opinion of David Taylor are reasonable.

Signed

Pamela Taylor

Rachel Taylor

Sarah Taylor

Jessica Taylor

Catherine Taylor

A triumph of theoretical hope over the reality of practical experience that all parents will understand. Here is evidence of David's application of his political creed of cooperation and participation in action. 'Inevitably,' Pamela told me, 'it didn't work.'

The family's animals still live on in the family home. It is a large rambling former rectory, situated immediately next to the churchyard in surprising seclusion even though it is located on Main Street in the village of Heather. It is shielded by trees from the highway and the schools and pub on the opposite side of the road. It is an ideal home for a large family. David's friend and former leader of the Leicester Council, Ross Willmott, recalls being one of the team of practical Co-operative Party members who carried furniture down Main Street to the third home that the Taylor family occupied in the same street.

In 2004 David wrote of the sobering thoughts of living next door to a village church for many years: 'One of my favourite poems is Thomas Gray's "Elegy written in a country churchyard".' He had no premonition of how soon Gray's words would accurately describe his own fate.

NEW LABOUR BLUES

The autumn gloom hit David in November 2002. The unrelenting battle with his in-tray drove him to a poetic parody. He told his constituents:

My apologies to those of you waiting for a reply to your correspondence, but I did do battle all day with an overloaded in-tray. I had just one brief outing to Donington-le-Heath Manor House for a re-enactment of early nineteenth century Navy life – inedible food, poor working conditions, strict commanding officers with harsh punishments. Not totally unlike the 2002 parliamentary regime.

In a backbench meeting with the Home Secretary I was critical of a penal policy which has doubled our prison population in a decade; in the Chamber I suggested to Gordon Brown that his figures on public debt didn't add up.

Received black looks from both ministers. Hope I haven't lost my only two friends in the Cabinet.

A midnight drive home for a Thursday Leicester Royal Infirmary visit. What a bleak month. No sun, no moon; No morn no noon; No garden flowers, no leisure hours; No time to while, no Chancellor's smile. November!

In his 'Parliament Patter' in early February 2003, he wrote of the 'grim spectre of war against Iraq that monopolised MPs mailbags'. David was still tribally loyal to Labour but he recognised the decisions on the Iraq War as above party considerations. The war punctured Tony Blair's reputation. David Taylor agonised. He wrote, 'A nightmare five-hour journey home slip-sliding up the M1. Fall asleep trying to understand the logic of government hawks who say we may need to destroy Baghdad in order to save it.'

There were other threats nearer home that enraged him. For thirty years he had been an impassioned campaigner against opencasting. When plans were announced for a new mine near his village, he issued his call to arms:

Planet Opencast is back. Back to rip up a mosaic of fields, hedges and trees running gently up towards Normanton Wood. We have been here before. Twice before in fact. Once bitten, twice shy, thrice defiant. Opencasting has been our history; it must not be our future. Locals tolerated it sixty years ago as our country needed energy to help rebuild an economy and a society stricken by long years of war.

We cannot put up with more noise, more dust and more heavy traffic. We shall fight against the eradication of ecology and loss of landscape. We cannot be bought by a few more trees and a few hectares more wetland. At the public inquiry later this year, Planet Opencast must be cast out into the long grass at the edge of the Universe.

Back in Parliament, he returned to national issues and
the most important vote of David's parliamentary career.
We all knew that our vote to take the UK into Bush's
war was to be one of the defining choices of the century.
Most Labour MPs sensed the possibility of defeat and
humiliation for Tony Blair. Two million angry protesters marched in London. The country was divided. The
Whips were in full battle cry. As usual their blandishments lacked subtlety. To me they tried to induce fear
by saying that Tony would resign if he failed to win the
vote. A general election was not an unwelcome prospect
in my case. I greatly enjoy elections – especially ones
when there is a chance to fight on matters on which I
have passionate views. Opposing the war in an election
victory might have avoided our involvement. Many
MPs had individual invitations to meet ministers.
Some were called to 10 Downing Street. It was the most
intense assault of bullying, bribery and blandishments
from the Whips that I have ever experienced. It worked.
Eighty Labour MPs who had expressed doubts and
opposition to the war were persuaded to abstain or vote
for war.

The Peter Pike table was divided. Gordon Prentice,
Ann Cryer and I were implacably opposed. Geraldine
Smith indulged in some deep heart-searching. She
argued that the secret services would not lie about
a threat from weapons of mass destruction. Lindsay
Hoyle was evenly poised but eventually voted for war.
David was greatly troubled but finally became persuaded
that the case for war was not proved. His diary records:

'On to the Chamber for the major debate on Iraq. I have received scores of constituents' e-mails in the last few days. Fine speeches on both sides, but the case put by ministers was unconvincing.'

David remained steadfast. He was one of the 139 'rebels' who defied the three-line whip. Hindsight has proved the wisdom of the rebellion. Had more Labour MPs rejected Blair's impassioned oratory, 179 brave British soldiers would have avoided death. An uncounted number of Iraqi lives would have been spared. The war is now seen as a Blair vanity mission that replaced one rotten Iraqi government with another rotten Iraqi government.

Tam Dalyell wrote later:

> David Taylor had a serious interest in foreign policy and agonised whether to support the government over the invasion of Iraq. He was one of those who voted against Blair in both February and March 2003, thereby extinguishing any hope that he may have had for ministerial preferment. He was a man of principle.

The tumultuous days of March 2003 were Parliament at its most intense. Had we been MPs for a hundred years there had never been a more vital decision. Previous generations had never voted on embarking on wars. The country had never been more divided and less convinced. To a greater degree than any other event, MPs judge their parliamentary worth by their votes on the Iraq war. David's analysis was calm, rational and objective. He did his duty as a Christian and a socialist.

COMPETITION SPUR

David had an energetic life outside of Parliament. He was devoted to riding his bike around the glorious Yorkshire Dales with a former fellow councillor David Bennett of Ashby. Yes, another David. I know of no explanation why the area was infested with people named David. In addition to David Taylor and his predecessor David Ashby there are his friends Canon David Jennings, David Bennett, David Farmer, David Wragg and David Drew.

David's passion for cycling was lifelong. He recalled:

My first bike was a Hercules New Yorker with white-wall tyres (which still stands at the back of our garage). Cycling is something which has stayed with me as a hobby and from the 1990s onwards I've continued my efforts as a long-distance cyclist covering such routes as the Pennine Way and Coast to Coast.

It does seem that that most basic form of transport – our own two feet – may be poised to make a comeback, if only for the sake of our health. I just hope that those who do take up walking enjoy the beautiful North West Leicestershire countryside rather than go to the gym. Getting from A to A on a treadmill seems a particularly pointless exercise to me!

David Bennett and David cycled coast to coast in August 2002 and, in September 2005, completed the Pennine Cycles Way from Appleby to Berwick-upon-Tweed. These are formidable challenges rich in drama. The two Davids were sharply competitive. Pamela cooperated but without a bike. David Bennett explains:

> She was morally supportive to David, and I was undermining. She had the thankless task of providing life support for two middle-aged males working through their midlife crises. She often spent hours waiting in lay-bys for us to arrive.

David Bennett has fond memories of his friend:

> Dave was a lovely human being. He demanded high standards of himself and was shocked that other people did not behave as he did. He would turn everything into a major project. We spent ages talking about rides but never properly planning anything. Then the wives of the two Davids, Pamela and Alison, would do the practical stuff, sort everything out at the last minute and phone the B&Bs.

They were great adventures.

> We started and finished the coast to coast over three days – Whitehaven to Tynemouth. The drill is to put the bike's back wheel into the sea one end and front wheel at the other end. It was in August 2002. We almost lost the

bikes down the slipway because it was pissing down with rain. As always Pam drove the car with bikes on the back.

David burnt himself out again and again. Ninety-nine per cent of the time he was ahead of me. One event was emblematic of our rides. Near Holme Firth, he got off the bike and said, 'I can go no further.' He should have packed it in miles earlier. It was just his grit and determination to be first that kept him going. We were rivals, friends. But mostly, kindred spirits.

His friends refurbished some legendary anecdotes about David's cricket prowess. The irrefutable facts are that he enjoyed middling success in the 1960s and 1970s as a medium-pace bowler in the Heather village cricket team. His best figures include an impressive seven wickets for nine runs against a Rolls-Royce team.

In the 1980s he competed as a long distance runner in many half-marathons and some marathons, completing the 1989 London Marathon in just over three hours.

David remembered to pack his competitive spirit in his luggage when he travelled to Coalville's twin town in France – Romans-sur-Isère in the Rhône-Alpes. He was part of the town-twinning group. Dutiful, as always, he took a keen interest in the entire programme including an exhaustive inspection of a local goat farm. He was off-duty and reasonably relaxed but his competitive animus was easily aroused and fiercely rampant. He had to win the game of boules. A simple introduction to a rare local sport became a key matter of national pride.

It was that same semi-rational desire to get to the

winning post first that propelled David into the sight of national television once a year. His impeccable Commons manners did not inhibit him from seizing every opportunity to maximise exposure. It was all in the good cause of ensuring his re-election and the continuation of the fine service his constituents enjoyed from him.

The eyes of the nation focus on Parliament during the annual ritual state openings. In one of David's regular newspaper columns, 'Parliamentary Patter', in December 2004 he pulled back the curtain of a parliamentary puzzle. There is a strict pecking order for the procession of MPs from the Commons Chamber to the House of Lords. Party leaders are first, followed by prominent frontbenchers. Humble backbenchers are consigned to the end of the procession and are unseen to the cameras in the Lords – except for David. Year after year he appeared among the leading group in full view of his admiring constituents nodding approval to the Prime Minister who was usually standing next to him.

David explained:

The state opening of Parliament – a day which included both magnificent spectacle and mindless speeches. When Black Rod summoned MPs for the Queen's Speech in the Lords, my sharp elbows got me into the front row to hear a long legislative list dominated by security and law and order issues. The dire and drab debate which followed indicates a late spring election. Draw the curtains and don't answer the door!

I believe 'sharp elbows' included some cunning positioning somewhere on the route, probably in the House
of Lords lobby. It's impossible to gatecrash the head
of the procession in the Commons. That would break
the long-established order of precedence. The Prime
Minister is coupled with the Leader of the Opposition;
the Foreign Secretary is accompanied by his shadow.
They try to make convincingly friendly small talk as
they parade before the cameras. Lowly interlopers have
no place in the first progress of the procession from the
Commons through the Central Lobby. Barging in as
the great and good bunch up to enter the Lords is possible. They are all too nice to object to this shameless queue
jumping. David was too coy to explain his technique to
the Peter Pike table. But we understood. Another ploy to
warm the cockles of his constituents' hearts.

It was not until 2012 that the House Authorities acted
to frustrate this shameless but harmless self promotion.
On 9 May an e-mail announced:

I have been contacted by a number of Members in
relation to preventing (or lessening) the sometimes
unseemly rush into the procession to the House of
Lords by Members who have not been in the Chamber.
Mr Speaker and both Chief Whips are in agreement
that jumping the queue is unfair on those Members
who have been in the Chamber for Prayers and for
Black Rod's summons.

At state opening today, the two division doors at the
bar end of the Chamber will be locked after Black Rod

enters to prevent Members queue jumping in front of the procession and that those Members in Members Lobby will be reminded that precedence will be given to Members coming from the Chamber.

Alas, the enterprise of the lowly was squashed. As ever, the mighty triumph: the humble are cast down.

AUDACIOUS GAMBLE

David was stung by an attack in the local press in 2004 complaining that MPs were wasting taxpayers' money. A letter in the *Coalville Times* irritated him greatly:

> For those that don't know, David Taylor gets a handsome salary of £1,160 per week and claims expenses of £2,500 per week. Yes, £2,500 per week! It's unbelievable. He's a nice bloke and an excellent constituency MP – but he isn't worth £3,660 a week to us.

David rashly announced his money-back guarantee: if constituents didn't approve of the job he was doing, they could claim their money back. He calculated that he cost each voter £4.80 a year.

The £5 offer alarmed most MPs as foolhardy. All politicians have thousands of political enemies eager to beggar them. Why give them such a chance? I believe my wife would regard such an offer by me as reckless – reason for divorce on the grounds of unreasonable behaviour. The thought of the large number of my constituents who might demand their money makes me feel queasy. David took a dreadful risk. He must have been supremely confident in his popularity and the stratospheric appreciation of the quality of his work.

'Oh, Dad,' groaned one of his daughters when she heard the news, 'isn't that just a little bit rash?' She had a point. Even if the offer was limited to households, there are just shy of 40,000 households in North West Leicestershire. He could have been bankrupted if a sizeable proportion of his 85,000 constituents took up the offer.

'Your daughter was right, wasn't she? Wasn't it a bit rash?' asked Lee Marlow, the *Leicester Mercury*'s political reporter. 'Well, I was sickened by this theory put forward by the newspaper,' David replied, 'that MPs pocket this money and blow it on living the high life. That's not true.'

David was outwardly confident. But I would not be surprised if he lost some sleep imagining an avalanche of demands arriving in the post. His friends worried on his behalf. David's instinctive honesty inhibited him from ignoring a routine journalistic jibe that would have soon been forgotten. He was on a mission to expose the whole truth.

To re-enforce the perception of his good value, he invited Lee Marlow to check on him and shadow him for a day in the Commons. Again, this was a gamble that could have backfired. I shared a hideous experience when I was working for an MEP. He had invited a local journalist to shadow him in Strasbourg. It was a disaster beyond imagination. My pacifist MEP, for complex reasons, became embroiled in a fight with a Tory MEP.

Pictures on the evening TV national news showed them rolling on the floor exchanging blows. The shadowing journalist faithfully reported the ugly details. The Lib Dems later used the footage in a party political broadcast to illustrate what they called 'a Labour MEP and a Tory MEP discussing foreign affairs'.

Happily David's guest saw nothing damaging. Lee's visit proved to be more an ordeal for him than a jaunt. He is a fine journalist armed with integrity. He explained to his readers:

The reason the *Mercury* is here today – sitting in on meetings and following David Leslie Taylor is simple. Respect for our politicians has diminished decade by decade and MPs are largely regarded as money-bagging sleaze monkeys with their snouts in the trough.

Today, we are riding shotgun with Mr Taylor to gauge just how hard working he really is. He works on average a seventy-five-hour week – forty or so hours during his four days in London and about thirty-five more when he is back on home soil. In the past year he has spoken 135 times in Parliament. Only four MPs have been more vocal.

He has attended 79 per cent of parliamentary votes ('It's lower than my previous record, but on some occasions I have been chairing committees or at constituency meetings') and is a familiar red-face in the Whips' office. He is the thirty-first most rebellious MP in the House of Commons.

Lee told me he was humbled by the exhausting experience of chasing David in an endless round of meetings. The diary was packed. It was an eye-opener for the man from the *Leicester Mercury*:

> I've been sticking like a limpet to David Taylor MP all morning and all afternoon. By 3pm, my bladder is telling me I haven't been to the toilet since I got up. Unless David Leslie Taylor has some kind of hidden catheter, he hasn't been either. This is the job where, literally, you don't get time to urinate.
>
> If you walked a day in his shoes, you would find it hard to begrudge him his £4.80 share of your income tax.

A month later David was grinning from ear to ear. His offer of refunding unhappy constituents had cost him just £50 rather than a whopping £200,000, which would have ruined him. Following his incredible announcement, David received only ten letters from disgruntled taxpayers – one of which was not even from his own constituency. He announced the response in one of his columns. He emphasised that the offer was 'now over'. The sense of relief is obvious.

In a statement on the take-up of his refund offer David said that he was tireless and that he worked 'non-stop for North West Leicestershire'. He declared that he had claimed £123,042 in expenses for the last financial year, on top of his £57,485 annual salary.

He told another newspaper that he employed three staff and 'ran himself ragged' for the people of the district. The paper had had the cheek to claim that his offer was a stunt. If it was, it was an extremely dangerous one that paid off, probably because of the widespread recognition of the truth of David's claim. He said it was an opportunity to access feedback from the community.

There is no danger that any other MP will repeat his offer – especially in these post-expenses scandal days. He brushed off cynical taunts of publicity seeking. He said it was 'merely an exercise in assessing his relationships with his constituents'. Possibly, or it may have been an intemperate burst of anger against a wounding jibe.

This was the first round of a bruising fight on MPs' expenses. David's gamble had paid off. The final round may have cost him his life.

The incident persuaded David to spell out his approach to some key difficulties facing politicos. MPs have constantly sought commandments for improving conduct. In 1997 I wrote Ten Commandments for my book *Commons Knowledge*. In 2012 following the expenses scandal I expanded these to thirty. David followed a different biblical list. There is a great deal of concentrated parliamentary wisdom in David's 'Seven Deadly Sins of Politics':

1. Anger – That we should debate national and local issues in a much less confrontational and high-octane manner. Grandstanding by MPs to the cameras and

radio has worsened things, as has a more partisan press which aims to portray complex matters in a black-and-white fashion.

Decisions should be taken without rancour or partiality. For while anger is never without an argument, it is rarely a good one. Nothing is more off-putting to the electorate than the yah-boo tendency.

2. Avarice – The philosopher Adam Smith was right to say that avarice and ambition are responsible for many of the world's injustices. Although 'limited avarice' may be an incentive to work and industry, we too often see it develop into an extreme greed for possessions; a position where a people's standard of living in a material sense squeezes out a country's quality of life in environmental and other ways.

Parliament frequently fails to flag up the long-term cost of short-term gratification.

3. Envy – That in a rampantly consumer society, the Tenth Commandment (thou shalt not covet...) still applies. Especially to those politicians who are the prisoners of envy in its most corrosive form.

These attempts to arouse the green-eyed monster or deepen discontent with our collective lot tend to be aimed at weakening public confidence in existing institutions without thinking through credible alternatives.

4. Gluttony – That politicians have too great an appetite for (well-meant) legislation, regulation and interference.

By pronouncing too confidently on every dispute, difficulty and dilemma we do a disservice to democracy. We raise hopes which, if dashed, are seized on as evidence of a widespread incompetence or uselessness in the political process.

5. Lust – That a legitimate political ambition for promotion or power can be corrupted and corralled by managers of (all) parties into a mindset that forbids independent thought or constructive criticism of one's own government. Loyalty is certainly vital and opposing views must be expressed in temperate language, but the belief that the electorate will be impressed by an outwardly united party heading in entirely the wrong direction (on major issues) is sadly, seriously mistaken.

6. Pride – Nothing alienates the general public more from politicians than if their arrogance and conceit is so clearly at odds with their abilities and conduct.

7. Sloth – That an unwillingness to work with others of different party persuasions on long-standing, deeply rooted political problems will often worsen the position.

Amen to all that.

STORMING THE BATTLEMENTS

David's tenuous loyalty to the New Labour brand was disappearing. He was falling out of love with Tony Blair. The Trident replacement was an irrelevant expensive provocation that David fiercely opposed. Things could only get worse. In 2005 Blair was looking for an eye-catching publicity stunt. He explained to the private meeting of Labour MPs that he planned to wrong foot the Tories with a demand for 92-day imprisonment without trial. Gleefully he claimed that anyone opposing this would be damned as 'pro-terrorist'.

It was a revolting stunt that cynically played on the public's fear after the summer bombings in London. There was outrage at the Peter Pike table. The Prime Minister was out of control. We all decided to vote against a grossly illiberal and unnecessary cheap stunt. It was a painful decision. David recalls a marathon thirty-two hour debate stretching from 1.30pm on Thursday until 7.30pm on Friday: bacon sandwiches, e-mails and catnaps kept MPs going through the longest parliamentary debate in nearly a hundred years. David managed to get 'a couple of hours' kip' in the House of Commons Library.

The government lost the vote because forty-nine
Labour MPs voted against. The new anti-terror proposals
were finally pushed through after a major government
climb-down.

David rebelled against the Bill until Tony Blair made
his final concession. The tabloid press excoriated all the
rebels as collaborators with terrorism. A few unfriendly
letters arrived from the tiny number of readers who
believed what they read in *The Sun*.

When the issue returned years later, the press had
lost interest. No one, not even Tony Blair, thought that
90-day detention was sensible or necessary. Backbench
sense defeated a cheap prime-ministerial stunt. Blair's
reputation was crumbling. David sublimated his anger
by reviving an old cause that was close to his heart.

Using the full armoury of the backbencher, David
introduced a Ten Minute Rule Bill. Only a dozen
of these have made it to the statute book in the past
twenty-five years. But they are great vehicles for raising individual concerns of MPs, gaining some publicity
and putting pressure on governments. David's fight for
fairness in education provoked the wrath of the Tory
national press.

David's Bill would have allowed teachers from
comprehensives to force their local grammar schools to
close. He told the Commons that parents would only
have a 'real choice' when all schools were comprehensive. He led a bid by 134 MPs – almost all Labour – to
outlaw Britain's remaining grammar schools.

The *Daily Express* squealed hypocrisy because their

'research' had discovered that David was educated at Ashby Boys' Grammar School in the late 1950s and early 1960s. This was an irrelevant non-revelation. It was no news to David's constituents or his fellow MPs who suffer earache from the number of times he had mentioned it.

David argued:

> What needs to be taken into account is the quality of secondary education on offer to the 75–80 per cent of children in the area who did not have access to the grammar school. Leicestershire went comprehensive in the late 1960s and has had a very good school system since then. I want to make good state comprehensives the natural choice for parents. It is a waste of the talents of the 80 per cent who miss out under the grammar school system if just 20 per cent are given greater resources and a better environment for learning.

The signed support of 134 MPs was formidable. But the government timidly refused to accept the unanswerable logic of David's argument. His call to dismantle current rules allowing local political activists to raise a petition to close their grammar schools was too radical for Blairites whose faith in the comprehensive system was feeble. One of Blair's acolytes had referred to 'bog-standard comprehensives'.

David was highly critical of the new procedures – 'a set of rules so structured that it is utterly impossible to ballot for change'. He said 'Kafka would have swooned

at the Byzantine complexity of it all. It is that deeply
flawed approach to consultation that my Bill seeks to
set aside.' He continued, 'The vacuous vacillation which
characterises the present arrangements is unsustainable.
The status quo must go.'

He won the vote by 132 votes to 105. But that was as
far as it went. Even a hollow victory is better than no
victory at all.

There was anger from on high when David attacked
foundation hospitals for threatening to undermine the
basic principles of the egalitarianism of the National
Health Service, but he was passionately defended in the
Leicestershire press. One reader spoke for a widespread
local view:

> Not for David Taylor the cosy government job and the
> climbing of the greasy pole. No, he's got his priorities
> right and this emblandishment [*sic*] or that inducement
> will have as much effect upon him as it does water on
> a duck's back. He deserves to be congratulated and
> should tell government's scolding whip that he repre-
> sents the people in North West Leicestershire and not
> the revamped conservatives who occupy the south east
> of England and who nowadays drive the policies of
> New Labour.
>
> The lad from Heather has always stuck by those
> who stand by him. Some, who would no more vote for
> David than they would throw themselves off the edge
> of Bardon Hill, recognise his achievements and grudg-
> ingly concede him to be an excellent advocate of their

aspirations and needs. Like yours truly, they realise that
in David Taylor you get what you see. A man who says
what he means and means what he says. How dare the
bully boys of government seek to reprimand him over
his stand on foundation hospitals.

On such powerful local support rebels are emboldened.
David's rebellions on most subjects were usually based
on deeply held convictions. Other issues troubled him.
He often long agonised, seeking a position that fairly
represented his constituents' interests. Three times he
voted to ban foxhunting but the hunters misinterpreted
his balanced view as weakness.

In his end of 2004 parliamentary report, he said
that there were 'greater priorities for legislation' such as
pensioner and child poverty and 'other aspects of animal
welfare' than the passing of the Hunting with Dogs Bill.
David had stronger views on animal laboratory experi-
ments. He added: 'For every fox killed by hunters in red
coats, there are 200 animals killed by experimenters in
white coats. Foxes could have waited.' Animal experimen-
tation had been a prominent issue in his constituency.

Experience proves that on these great divisive issues
it is dangerous to appear undecided. The restless zealots
of both arguments will swarm the MPs and make life
hell. In their campaigning strategies they divide MPs
into 'for', 'against' and 'those who can be persuaded'.
The hunters threatened to target David to unseat him
in the general election. David replied, 'I think the threat
will backfire on them. If the countryside is highlighted

as an issue in North West Leicestershire, I believe it will bring out the Labour vote.'

David flinched in horror when he was wooed by Lembit Öpik, who offered the snake oil solution of the Middle Way Group. Funded by the hunting fraternity, they claimed to have invented a compromise to the ban on killing foxes by hunting with dogs. What was it? Hunting with cats? Half-killing a fox?

David sent him packing.

DAVID TAYLOR VOTE

One permanent legacy that David bequeathed to Parliament is the David Taylor vote.

Professor Philip Cowley has spoken of his exasperation with David. Philip chronicles and interprets parliamentary votes. David frequently wrecked his arithmetic. When 540 MPs voted, how was it that 500 voted aye and forty-one voted no? It was David's fault for voting twice. While there may have been previous occasions when MPs voted in both lobbies, it was David who challenged the system with carefully considered abstentions.

By 2008 David had the tenth most rebellious record for voting against the government. He said he had never caved in to Whips, Home Secretaries or even Prime Minister Gordon Brown.

He bristled over Tory taunts that he had been bullied into a vote by the Labour Prime Minister. He blasted back: 'I was under no pressure from Gordon Brown. He has no leverage on me. I'm a backbencher who is standing down in two years time – he can't have anything on me.'

The *Leicester Mercury* reported:

the 'yes-no' tactics of David – who voted FOR and
AGAINST the Counter Terrorism Bill – seem to have
caused much excitement locally.

Mr Taylor didn't waste a second last night on round-
ing on local Conservatives. They were hair-dryered
for daring to suggest he had 'misled' his constituents for
failing to oppose the government's controversial terror
detention plan, which won a nail-biting 315 votes to 306.

David thundered:

After the 42-day debate, I cast a positive abstention –
voting in both lobbies – as I was unconvinced by the
government's case, but nauseated by the Tory hypocrisy
in opposing it. I didn't give any assurances about voting
against it – only voting for it.

The would-be Tory MP for the district, Andrew Bridgen,
said that despite assurances to local constituents that
he would vote against the bill, the MP had taken the
unusual step of voting twice – effectively abstaining
from the vote.

Since his first election in 1997 David became increasingly rebellious. In the first Blair term he cast only five
dissenting votes. It was thirty-nine in the second and
seventy-six times in the 2005–10 parliament. He went
from being the joint seventy-second most rebellious MP
in 1997–2001 to being the eighth in his final parliament.

His deep faith led him to vote in a socially conservative direction when it came to matters of conscience.

It was unfortunate that the Whips imposed their will on some of these delicate issues. Kelvin Hopkins recalls his surprise discussing key votes with David Drew and David Taylor, then watching them both wander a little sheepishly into the 'wrong' lobby, which was shunned by his Campaign Group comrades. The two Davids shared similar religious convictions.

In July 2005 *Mail* journalist Quentin Letts observed a telling incident:

> I was eyewitness two days ago to an intriguing confrontation in the Commons. A Labour whip Gillian Merron entered the Chamber and made a beeline for an excellent, independent-minded Labour MP David Taylor. She handed him a hand-written note and forced him to read it in front of her. Doing so, he exhibited all the gestures of a man being menaced by the secret police.
>
> Dark, dangerous Miss Merron patted his knee in an unloving fashion and left Mr. Taylor to shake his head repeatedly and to stew in his own juices. Later that night he voted against the government twice in the Religious Hatred Bill.

Dissenting votes were cast by David on matters as diverse as the deregulation of the gambling industry and whether clergymen should be allowed to exercise free speech when it came to expressing their opposition to homosexuality. One dissenting vote was on 2 December. It was a vote for an amendment to the Equality Bill that would have provided exemptions for religious organisations in employment matters on grounds of sexual orientation.

To the great majority of MPs a vote is a reflex action. They troop into the lobby pointed to them by the sheepdog Whips. To David, each vote was a personal vote only marginally influenced by the Whips. He was not the first to vote in both lobbies but he stamped his name on this useful device. He did it in earnest and registered no fewer than thirty-three deliberate abstentions in 2005–10 alone. The last one was on 8 December 2009 in protest at government policy on disability benefits for the elderly.

Professor Philip Cowley wrote in sorrow that 'casting our eyes over divisions lists in the present parliament, there will be a huge gap, not just in the ayes and noes lobbies but where David Taylor's name was often to be found in both lobbies'.

The legacy is that MPs can now use an abstention vote thanks to David's precedents.

RENAISSANCE OF A REBEL

There was fevered speculation before the 2005 election. The press reported that results in the four Leicestershire seats could play a crucial role in deciding the national result. The shine had worn off Tony Blair. There was deep anger from Labour voters against the war in Iraq.

The local Conservatives announced their top targets were the Labour seats of Loughborough and North West Leicestershire. David had already privately told Pamela that he was thinking of standing down as an MP. He was persuaded to stay because of his local strength as a vote magnet. He knew that this would be his last parliament.

In one of his regular columns David mused:

> Does some odd symmetry suggest this is my last ever *Echo* column? Can I thank readers for their comments and interest in it over the years, which I have much appreciated. Au revoir or goodbye? Only time (and turnout) will tell.

The expected collapsing turnout was his main neurosis. Canvassing was dispiriting. The loyalty to David was still solid but the contempt for warmonger Blair ran deeply especially among the Labour faithful. Many threatened to send a message to Blair by voting Lib Dem or by abstaining.

David's opponent was the lively Nicola Le Page who scented victory. She ran a competent campaign. Her supporters warned her off attacking David because his reputation made him almost unassailable. David probably privately agreed. But it was a nail-biting count. Several times during the evening, Labour and Tory were running neck and neck as the votes were counted. The *Mercury* reported:

> A small cheer greeted Nicola le Page as she arrived at about 12.45am. In a smart black suit and killer heels, she had a confident air and for a while, it looked like she might just pull it off. Mr. Taylor allowed himself to smile only after it was clear he had won – spending the long hours leading up to the result looking anxious and tense.

The final result was reassuring. The local swing from Labour to Tory was 4.3 per cent compared with the national swing of 5.5 per cent. David had again scored above the party's national vote. Labour's majority in the Commons was slashed from 160 to sixty-six, largely due to the disillusionment with Blair's subservience to Bush in sending our soldiers to die in pursuit of non-existent weapons of mass destruction.

Relieved by his majority of 4,477, David surprised everyone with his victory speech. He called for Tony Blair to stand down, minutes after he accepted his seat for a third consecutive term. He said: 'I call for a leadership change and I will support that change.' Simultaneously Labour's big guns of former Foreign Secretary Robin Cook and ex-Health minister Frank Dobson made similar comments.

David also paid conventional thanks for his hat-trick: 'It's a huge privilege for me to be selected by my own party for four successive elections in my home patch. I am delighted to be here to serve for the third time in a row.'

The presence of the BNP candidate and his supporters was low-key until David attacked them. Their members booed and retaliated with: 'You have blood on your hands.' The BNP candidate and supporters left in the middle of David's speech, seemingly in disgust, booing and catcalling as they went.

David was upset that an extremist party had garnered 1,474 votes in his beloved constituency and former mining area. He said, 'The representation of a dangerous fifth party in this constituency is a clear threat to future democracy.'

In his first newspaper column a week later he wrote:

It's back to work again after election victory... The strife is o'er, the battle done; Now is the Victor's triumph won; O let the song of praise be sung; Alleluia.

The speaker cars are silenced, the posters removed from roadside verges and the flow of leaflets through letterboxes had dried up. But the conflict has only moved from the constituencies to Westminster...

This was a different David to the idealistic newcomer of 1997. Eight years at the parliamentary wordface had reduced his high expectations and increased his wish for practical results. In his final parliament he intended to rely on his backbench initiatives rather than expect government reforms which would never arrive. Winding down was not David's way. Winding up was his incurable trait. He accelerated his work, hungry for achievements as his time in Parliament diminished.

In a speech after the state opening, he told the House about local successes in crime prevention. This was David the county councillor on stilts:

> My constituents have not stood idly by waiting for effective government action on crime. Three years ago, we resolved to tackle the roots of crime rather than just wringing our hands and calling for harsher sentences. We believed that, unless we acted, we would all take some blame for crime in our society. Acquiescence would merely be guilt by default.

He described the local forum that was doing detailed hard-headed work in the high crime micro-areas such as Ashby town centre. He had helped set up a youth council that was 'a grey-suit-free zone' so that the young would have a real say:

> When they speak, we must listen, and when their demands are reasonable, we must respond. If we begin to nod because boredom or intolerance has set in, the

time will have come to examine our behaviour because we shall be contributing to the alienation of the young.

He also sought a practical improvement to tackling the immense misery caused by dementia. He quoted Einstein:

> The intuitive mind is a sacred gift, and the rational mind its faithful servant. We have created a society that honours the servant and has forgotten the gift.

He accused governments of various colours of forgetting the gift by concentrating on researching cancer and heart disease and neglecting dementia. He had introduced a Ten Minute Bill on the management of dementia in care homes. One of its objectives was to make dementia training, including the use of antipsychotics, mandatory for care home staff.

His arguments were striking. In every MP's constituency there were about a thousand people suffering from dementia. Overuse and misuse of neuroleptics was the nation's greatest drug scandal. Tens of thousands were suffering misery and confusion in their final days for administration convenience or to reduce staff costs. He said, 'In many instances anti-psychotics were prescribed to treat behaviour that is neither distressing nor threatening, such as restlessness or being vocal – often basic expressions of need.'

Realistic crime fighting and giving a voice to the silent in residential homes for the elderly were causes worthy of David's energies for his final term.

HEAVEN VIA HELL

Squeezed into David's absurdly busy schedule of parliamentary work were mini oases of time devoted to family holidays. He confesses to one slip from his path of perfection: a rare day of parliamentary truancy on 2 March 2000. He writes in his newspaper column, 'Parliamentary Patter':

> Early tour around the Palace of Westminster by a large group of children from Albert Village school who are on a short visit. Much enjoyed talking to them, their parents and teachers. The final primary school teacher visitor of the week was my eldest daughter Rachel who is down to see the Dome with her fiancé Jon. A pleasant relaxing afternoon (don't tell anyone) – no phone calls, meetings, letters, e-mails. Bliss.

At election times there was just one Labour Party poster in the town of Sheringham, the seaside town on the unspoilt, unfashionable Norfolk coast. It was not in the two-up, two-down cottage that the Taylor family rented. They were not that organised. But even one poster was a comfort. It meant that their favoured holiday destination was not in entirely hostile political territory. But there is no Labour Party in Sheringham. David hoped to combine his precious family time with some political missionary work in his long-planned future of semi-retirement.

Daughter Jessica welcomed David's promised less frantic approach to his duties:

> In more recent years it was nice to get him away from North West Leicestershire for a holiday so that he could relax. We went to Sheringham, Cornwall and Center Parcs in Sherwood Forest. He would have time to doze on the sofa and cover the floor in newspapers. He would always buy several different newspapers, tabloid and broadsheet, so he could see what was being read by the electorate.

Sheringham modestly describes itself as the 'Jewel of the North Norfolk Coast'. It boasts half a dozen pubs and restaurants catering for all tastes, from fish and chips to first-class cuisine. There are four blue plaques. One marks the home of celebrated composer Ralph Vaughan Williams. Another commemorates the 'site of a fisherman's hut'. The understated tourist trap was the perfect holiday habitat for the understated politician. It is also located 133 miles from Heather. That was usually enough to separate David from the insatiable demands of constituency work on his time. Daughter Catherine also shares fond memories of Sheringham as a calm refuge where David could be at the untroubled heart of family fun.

Another frequent undemanding destination was the Croyde Bay holiday centre in Devon. The Taylor family were entitled to a hefty discount because David was a veteran member of the National and Local Government Officers' Association (NALGO). It was in the latter years that Sheringham became the favoured destination.

Only once did the lure of an unmissable constituency event persuade him to take the 266-mile round trip back to Heather. It was a diary foul-up. He had agreed to open the Heather village flower show. That was an unbreakable promise. Other MPs are baffled by this excessive devotion to constituency minor events. But that was David.

His refusal to fly confined the family to road or rail to reach their beloved France. Their preferred sites were in the Brittany forests. They would 'camp' on sites where the tents were already erected. They had a seven-seater vehicle and the organisation was like a military campaign. Pamela recalls that he objected to early-morning laziness and woke everyone up before they were ready to face the day. She said:

> We would go off to the markets and all the other attractions. Often we arrived at attractions when they were closing. David seemed able to visualise the maps and was never wrong. When we got lost it was my fault. We had great times and became regular customers to all the ferry ports including Santander.

Jessica remembers the trial of having a bossy father:

On family holidays he would stride off, leading the way with me and my sisters walking somewhere in the middle and my mum bringing up the rear. On summer holidays we often went to France and would stay on several campsites. On changeover days he would want to make an early start on the drive from one campsite to another. He wanted to get on the roads before they got too busy.

Not far into one journey Catherine became unwell and we had to stop to sort her out. Dad was not particularly sympathetic and was annoyed at the delay. Then a lorry passed by us on the road and he angrily said, 'Here come the lorries.' This became a family catchphrase that would often be repeated when he was rushing too much or surrendering to his Stalinist tendencies. Perhaps the car sickness was due to Dad's driving style!

Being a passenger in a car driven by David was an experience most people never forgot.

David often rhapsodised about his abiding minor vice, his love affair with cars:

At nineteen, I learned to drive and my first vehicle was a Ford Thames Van – 8545 HP (registration number, not the loan required!). Motoring offered freedom from the chains of bus timetables and fear of missing the last bus home after a night out, but at a cost. A personal cost in the pocket and an environmental cost to society as a whole as increased car ownership led to increasingly congested roads and an increasingly polluted atmosphere before global warming had even been thought of.

His best remembered car was a Capri with a 2.8 big engine. The kindly Alan Costello said, 'You could not get in his car it was such a mess. He was the worst driver in the world.'

A fellow Labour Party worker said:

He was a terrible driver, and an incessant talker. He would be wandering over the white line. He typically had a pie or a chunk of bread on the dashboard. He was permanently in election mode. His timetable was always impossible. There was never enough time to fit everything in – so he ate at the wheel. Stopping to eat would have been a sinful waste of canvassing or 'meeting the people' time and an impediment in his campaign to become omnipresent. It was always a relief to arrive at a destination. After their first experience as David's passenger most people would insist, 'Next time, I'll drive.'

His friend Bob Underwood suggested a possible role model for his unnerving driving:

Our friendship really blossomed in the early 1970s when I recall being driven home from a meeting in Loughborough. The car was a Morris Marina and the driver was the late councillor Wilson Todd. He drove in a manner akin to Mr Toad and in the process caused David and I to scream for our lives.

Another old friend claimed that David believed that no other traffic should be on the road or anywhere else competing with him. He described the experience of approaching a field where a light aircraft used for spraying pesticides was taking off. David took up the challenge and raced it in his old Ford Van. He was level with the plane at the end of the field when it took off.

David had no speeding convictions that anyone could remember. There was an incident in an election campaign when he was observed doing 30 mph while talking on his mobile phone as he passed a school. That got him into a bit of trouble. He was very repentant.

His family are a tad more generous but the verdict is the same. He was intolerant with delays. Jessica explains:

> He was a very busy man and therefore was always in a rush. He always had many social engagements to attend. His driving was somewhat scary at times. Before it became compulsory, it was a challenge to get him to wear a seatbelt; he would claim that if he wore it he would drive even faster than he already did.

His staff went to great lengths to avoid going in a car with him. They all shuddered and painted a picture of his driving a car at high speed while eating a sandwich and while his head was trying to solve the world's major crises. Some even alleged he combined driving with reading a newspaper and consuming a bacon sarnie.

That qualifies him as a hell-driver.

POROUS SHELL-BACK

David Taylor was the kindest and most inoffensive of human beings. He talked, thought and behaved like an experienced mature MP but he did not posture or preen as most MPs do.

Canon David Jennings perceptively describes the self-effacing, genuinely modest David Taylor:

> If you were at a reception or a party or in a room with him, you could have a conversation with him about all sorts of issues and you could come away and not know he was an MP. Whereas others I'm sure would want to tell people that I'm a Member of Parliament, I'm a Lord or I'm a whatever. Many people met the North West Leicestershire MP without knowing it.

On the other hand, he was always generous when introducing others. 'He always said some very complimentary things about me, about how he looked to me as a bit of a mentor on the council,' David Jennings explained. 'And he'd say to other people "this man actually taught me". I was always humbled by that.'

His colleagues and staff sing a hallelujah chorus of praise about the joy of his company. Former MP David

Drew fondly recalled his habitual cheery greeting, 'How is Mr Drew? And Mrs Drew? And all the little Drews?'

In the interests of balance and credibility, I have sought out some weaknesses that reveal him to be a human being and not a saint.

It was not easy. Eventually I found one example of possible self-serving vanity that casts a doubt over his case for canonisation. His car had a DLT number plate, David Leslie Taylor! It was a big car, which may have been previously owned by Dave Lee Travis. Some explained it away as an element in David's service to his community by announcing his omnipresence! Canon Jennings identifies it as a lapse that proves the universality of narcissism. A member of his staff added that it also 'showed off his racy driving habits'. Two foibles combined!

There was always a minute dribble of carping criticism of David in the local press. No more than all MPs suffer and always trumped by appreciative letters. But there was some consternation, which weighed heavily on David, when a prominent national personality attacked him.

A memorial stone was about to be unveiled in his constituency in 2005 to commemorate two police officers who had been killed on duty. David Taylor was eager to honour the memories of Bryan Moore and Andrew Munn. They had died when their police vehicle was hit by a car that was being chased by another police car. David was upset by the tragedy and he wished to show his respects. This was another 'David Taylor' issue. He was on very good terms with the local police and his sympathy was deep and genuine.

To his great credit, Michael Winner was mainly responsible for funding and running a charity that erected memorials to policemen killed on duty. A stone was to be unveiled at a service station, on the M1 close to the scene of the incident. The two officers were also remembered with a memorial garden, officially opened at Leicestershire Police headquarters in Enderby.

For reasons that still remain something of a mystery, there was an administrative foul-up that convinced Michel Winner that David was not answering invitations to the event promptly enough. He was abusive to David's staff in a phone-call. An experienced staff member was reduced to tears. He then sent a remarkable fax to David on 1 July 2005 saying, inter alia, 'In the twenty-year history of the Police Memorial Trust no one has behaved in a manner of the great pig other than you … You are a total arsehole.' The odd turn of phrase 'great pig' is burnt in the memory of David's staff. Very curious. Entirely mistaken.

David was shaken by this bizarre insult from a nationally known personality. Colourful insults appear to be a habit of the accuser. It was not only David who angered him. Later he refused to accept an OBE – again with little grace – because it was the appropriate award for a 'toilet cleaner at King's Cross'.

David had grown his own shell back to protect him from the insults and blows that hammer all politicians. But his was porous. He was vulnerable to suffer deeply from wounds that would be pinpricks to more resilient politicos. He was eventually persuaded that a meaningless insult was a matter of little consequence. No one was very interested and the incident is now forgotten and invisible even on the encyclopaedic prairies of Google's past news.

His spirits soon returned to their happy equilibrium. Proof that David was securely lodged in the affections of his constituents was the self-mocking tone of his newspaper columns. In the shark-infested waters of politics it is dangerous to display wounds or weaknesses. Political opponents are poised to strike.

By 2005, David was fearless and indifferent to the possibility of mockery. Why should he care what his opponents might say? No one mocked David as skilfully or engagingly as he mocked himself. Rashly he promised to avoid alliteration in future. It was another hostage to fortune and a promise he could not keep.

He published his 2005 resolutions on the basis of another dodgy theory:

The more people who know of my resolutions, the more likely it is that I will not be able to shred them quietly on 6 January, along with the cards and Christmas tree.

No.1.   Ditch my habit of always saying yes. No more shall I agree (almost always in a weak moment) to write articles for national magazines with readerships that would barely fill a minibus. Never again address far-away meetings with a tiny audience of a lost dog and the secretary. When asked if her members had been told I was coming, she said 'No, but it must have got out.'

No.2. Discard my tendency to procrastinate. The success of the website last minute.com was no surprise at all to people like me. Taylor's Law states that if it weren't for the last minute nothing would ever get done. Right from school, where I needed the adrenalin created by imminent examinations to revise in earnest, through a working life punctuated by just achieved dead-lines, I have been dogged by this character flaw. Decisions are delayed, plans are postponed. I am hoping to found a group at Westminster for MPs similarly afflicted.

No.3. Dispose of my old technology. I really am not one of those people who believe that modern technology owes ecology an apology. Having spent three decades in software development before 1997, I hope I have been the very opposite of a technophobe. Nevertheless, I seem to have spent the last eight years becalmed in a technological cul-de-sac. My mobile phone is the size and weight of a house brick. My 2004 appointments have been scrawled in an increasingly bedraggled pocket diary. My computers would be at home in a science museum and my music is still on cassettes. Sad, eh?

No.4. Drop my surplus excess pounds. I blame a local newspaper. A recent photograph showed a very stark profile – the heavy impact wreaked by an MP's work on my formerly sylph-like frame. No longer can I fool myself that modern suits must shrink after frequent dry-cleaning. Whether in North West Leicestershire or in London, a typical week can contain several receptions with savoury refreshments. The weight of nibbles and volumes of drinks consumed at such affairs can seriously depress you on your bathroom scales.

No.5. Dump the parliamentary rhetoric. We all have pet hates. My own include the way in which our mother tongue is more and more mangled and manipulated. If I hear anyone else say 'I love so and so to bits' I think I will scream. Or see a poster saying such and such is provided 'for free'; I shall be sorely tempted to strike out the first word with a highlighter pen. But hearing myself on recorded radio clip using old clichés like 'raising our game', 'long-awaited report' and 'best practice targets' really was the 'last straw'. From now on it's always going to be plain speaking. No more meaningless jargon. And no more alliterative groups of five items like the above list!

Some of the resolutions were attainable. Ending alliteration was not.

THE GLORY AND THE MESS

The rule is that no MP is a hero to the staff they employ.

The relationship is unrelenting and claustrophobic when two or three staff share the hothouses of small offices pressurised with big demands from the public and the media. MPs are peculiar people, demanding and usually infuriating megalomaniac bosses. David's staff were exceptionally open with me on the thrilling, demented, uplifting chaos of coping with David. A couple of muffled hints about David's trying conduct as an employer were heard. There was no severe criticism but a little irritation at his reluctance to delegate.

A perceptive assessment of David as a boss came from Matt Mulley, his greatest fan and his sharpest critic:

> His standards were never too high for his staff. They were too high for him. There was never any work I did that he was critical about other than in a constructive way. Maybe the standards he expected from other MPs or other people were too high but as for his staff – it was fine.
>
> To work with him was incredibly frustrating. He was disorganised and late and didn't listen to things. We

tried for months and months to get him a meeting with Kitty Ussher when she was Department for Work and Pensions minister. We finally got fifteen minutes with her. He didn't turn up – because he forgot, or because he was talking to someone else but wouldn't say 'look I have to go'. He wouldn't let anyone down, deliberately, but he could not please everyone.

David combined two of the worst features of a fellow office worker. He was endemically untidy and an incurable hoarder. Nothing was ever thrown away. The mess was a torment for those cursed with tidy minds. The perpetual growth of the mass of papers and reports was worse. The piles encroached daily into the cramped working space. There was a filing system but it existed only in David's head. There was no logic to it that any of his staff could penetrate.

He was also a chronic procrastinator. Trivia absorbed too much of his attention. Matters of world importance would often be neglected because he was excessively preoccupied with issues of protozoan insignificance. It is an infuriating trait for staff eager to solve the big problems of the planet.

Part of David Taylor's law is that 'if it weren't for the last minute nothing would ever get done'. David's staff were unanimous in seething about his belated demands. His daughter Jessica confirms that she has inherited his trait of 'leaving things until the last minute and therefore rushing to finish tasks, as though adrenalin is required for their completion'.

Coping with David's eccentricities was often trying for staff. His anti-flying phobia restricted activities and added another headache for those who had the tedious ticklish jobs of booking trains across Europe to destinations that coincided with the arrival of other MPs who had flown to meetings of the Council of Europe.

Lauren Otter pinpointed David's main weakness:

He couldn't delegate! And the other problem was the small total of male staff because at first he couldn't manage male staff. That's why his office in the early years was full of women. I think he found it easier to ask a woman to do something. I'm not implying that he meant we were servants or anything dreadful. Just that it was easier to tell a woman 'I want it like this'. Maybe we were more inclined to do it the way he wanted.

It is a curiosity of parliamentary life that many MPs are uncomfortable employing people of their own sex. The clash of macho egos can disrupt the smooth running of all-male MPs teams. Female rivalry may prove neuralgic in offices of women MPs. Who knows? But that's the way it is with a surprising percentage of MPs.

I asked Daniel Crimes about David's technique for preparing for his renowned oral questions. Did he or his staff write them?

David would ask me to gather material on whatever subject he was working on. I'd trawl the press for any contemporary issues on the current subjects of controversy. The charm of his interests was that they were wide-ranging and sometimes random. But he was always quite flexible. He was a rarity. He had a witty penetrating aphorism for almost every situation that arose on the vast parliamentary agenda.

David did not want to be labelled a usual suspect. But he was determined to hold the government to account. He knew that the prime role of a backbencher was to hold the government's feet to the fire. But his chronic kindness broke through. He was reluctant to wound the answering minister and he habitually blunted the sharp insults that his staff suggested.

Daniel Crimes worked for David in Westminster for nine years. His ambition was to lighten some of the burdens of David's work and strengthen his parliamentary persona. Daniel has worked for many MPs. Like all of them, David would demand information at the last moment. Like few of them, he was never unreasonable in his expectations nor was he resentful when things went wrong.

Daniel recalls with affection:

He was my longest-term employer. He was thoroughly decent, generous, very conscientious, and always aware of an employee's needs, always worried that he might be putting his employees under too much pressure. Perhaps he became self-defeating in his excessive concern for others.

His humour was a delight. He was hilarious! I remember him telling me that when he first arrived, he and Stephen Pound had a short but extremely amusing exchange of wit and wisdom. I really do miss him. If only he were here now laying waste to these new Tories!

In the Chamber David's humour was sometimes contrived but often spontaneous. Humour can be a dangerous minefield. He had the ability to think on his feet but occasionally rushed in and upset a few excessively sensitive souls. He asked the Olympics minister Tessa Jowell if additional events would be included in the 2012 games to encourage greater participation from Essex competitors:

> Will the minister care to deny the scurrilous rumours that, to encourage the people of Essex to be more involved, it is intended that the sports of putting the medallion and throwing the white high heels should be included?

This piece of innocuous light banter was picked up by a hack who was a fierce defender of Essex nationalism or, perhaps, having a quiet day. He rang Lord Hanningfield, the Conservative leader of Essex County Council, and invited him to rage against David.

He grabbed the bait and said 'we have moved on from the tired stereotypes of twenty years ago and I suggest Mr Taylor does the same'.

This was not one of David's best jokes, but forced pomposity discourages the odd flashes of fun and colour in turgid parliamentary exchanges.

Lauren Otter's voice betrayed strong emotion in summing up her years working with David:

He was a great employer, absolutely first class. He did everything by the book. In a small constituency office with a limited budget it must have been tempting to get somebody other than me. They were some of the best years of my working life. My inspiration is entirely David's example as a serving politician. David genuinely and substantially helped people. That was his wholehearted commitment and what could be better than that?

David was reluctant to endure the purgatory of employing staff through advertisement, interviews and the choice of one and the painful rejection of many. Matt Mulley's appointment to David's office was serendipity:

I met him by accident. I was desperately trying to get into the House of Commons. I think I'd made eighty-five applications – for internships, for jobs, just offering my work for free, everything!

By chance I had an invite to a Commons dinner. I sat down next to a sort of crumpled, dishevelled slightly absent-minded guy. He seemed a bit space cadet-ish. He had half his dinner on his lapels. We got talking, somehow without exchanging the 'what do you do' conversation.

Soon we were into a really deep conversation about education. Halfway through the dinner, the bell rang and he disappeared. It was only then that I realised he was an MP. He gave me his card and told me to keep in touch if I wanted to. I wrote to him and to my eternal surprise he wrote back and we carried on corresponding about politics and policy stuff for about two months.

David couldn't offer Matt a job. His staff budget was already overstretched. But he had his usual difficulty in saying no to anyone. He was always trying to pay too many people. He offered to pay Matt's expenses and give him an internship for as long as he wanted, whenever he wanted.

Matt's employers refused him time off or even leave without pay. In the end he abandoned his job, took out a loan to pay his rent for six months and went to work for David on the gamble that he would get a job eventually. Within six weeks, on David's recommendation, he got a part-time job working for fellow Labour MP Anne McGuire. Later on, David found the cash to give him a part-time job too.

That was not the end of the uncomfortable bed Matt had made for himself. He worked for two MPs out of one office. They were both very flexible but the work was a bewildering challenge. David and Anne are at the opposite ends of the Classic Labour and New Labour spectrum. For Matt the process was educational. He was in the middle with the two of them pulling him from either side.

Matt offered his unqualified tribute to David, which suggested the title of this book:

He had more integrity that anyone I've ever met. He was also unfailingly generous, of spirit, financially and with his time. He really gave of himself; his heart and soul went into everything. If he had any weakness it was his inability to say no.

BACKBENCHER OF THE YEAR

There are no tangible rewards for the successful backbencher. Top ministers have many. The backbencher accolades awarded by fellow MPs are greatly prized.

David was shortlisted for the Backbencher of the Year award in 2006 and 2007. He missed the title in 2006 but was more hopeful in 2007 when he was shortlisted along with three other formidable parliamentarians: Norman Baker, Edward Leigh and Patrick Mercer.

To the acclamation of the Peter Pike table, David triumphed. The event is organised by Sky TV and *The House* magazine, and the result decided by a ballot of the 650 MPs. The citation described him as 'an indefatigable campaigner. A constant attender and independent-minded.' Parliament's own ePolitix website described him as a 'regular thorn in the side of ministers'.

David's words and demeanour expressed his genuine modesty. He said:

It was a real privilege to be on the shortlist of four for the second time and a wonderful surprise to have won this year. I am most grateful for the support of colleagues in all parties. Like all backbenchers I try to hold the government to account on behalf of my constituents, and to steer a line between mindless obedience and persistent rebellion.

It's important that ministers hear from all sides of the Chamber constructive criticism of the departments for which they are responsible. Many backbenchers do this on a daily basis – I am fortunate to have been chosen on this occasion.

His words added fresh lustre to his reputation and confirmed the wisdom of his fellow parliamentarians in making him Backbencher of the Year 2007.

That week, a sketch writer underlined David's qualifications for the award by describing how David used his subtle wit to puncture the pretensions of a self-regarding prima-donna frontbencher. Quentin Letts wrote:

It was at this moment that David Taylor, a rather hairy Labour MP who sits on the furthermost back bench, stood up to say that there will be great joy in the City of London that Mr Milburn has decided to spend more time with his government. MPs tittered for it is true that only last year Mr Milburn insisted that he must leave Cabinet to spend more time with his family. Clearly something has changed, though no one is sure what.

Mr Taylor said that he wants Mr Hain to find time in the Commons timetable for Mr Milburn to explain his policies. In particular Mr Taylor wants to hear about Mr Milburn's 'touching belief that great amounts of private money and private influence are necessary to drive up standards in public services'.

Being Backbencher of the Year adds kudos and authority to the elected one. The Peter Pike table raised a small glass of finest Rioja selected by Kelvin Hopkins to toast our worthy hero. There were appreciative murmurs from friends and foes in the Chamber and new wariness from ministers nervous of the master backbencher's barbs. The Leicestershire press were generous in their reporting. Thrilled constituents purred with pleasure at a national accolade for 'our David'.

MYTHS, SORCERY AND OTHER ACCOUNTING DEVICES

D avid's best speech was on the Private Finance Initiative (PFI). He called the debate in July 2001 when Gordon Brown was the almost unchallenged colossus of financial policy.

The myth of cheap money for instant political gratification was the accepted un-wisdom of most MPs of all parties. The bills would have to be paid later. PFI was like a national Ponzi rip-off. David spoke with his routine brilliance. The language is vivid, the arguments are penetrating. The minister Paul Boateng replied with a complacent superficial civil service handout that side-stepped the unanswerable case David made. The transient vacuities of Boateng won him a glittering political career. The wisdom of David secured him a respected pedestal in the gallery of honoured courageous Cassandras.

Kelvin Hopkins described the speech as 'magnificent'. I quote it at full length because David said it was the speech that he would like to be judged by in the year 2020. It is the essence of all his talents: witty, prophetic, authoritative and delivered with engaging, relaxed, persuasive aplomb. Many parliamentary speeches rely on briefing from outside specialists. Every word in this speech is original David Taylor.

In the world of politics that now demands sound bites and pithy questions, David excelled. But he also had the depth of serious purpose that enabled him to make a speech that had all the characteristics which have been admired for centuries in Parliament. No media will now report more than a sentence or two on a speech of this length. But this one had a profound effect on those who heard it in the Chamber or on television. Time has been kind to his views. In 2001 they were unfashionable in the shallow hollow world of New Labour and cowardly Conservatism. This speech brilliantly demonstrated that the emperors Blair and Brown had no clothes. Their canards have been found wanting by all independent commentators.

As a public-sector accountant I must confess dismay and astonishment at the readiness of my government to prod and coerce public agencies down the PFI and public-private partnership route using a rationale that is frequently dubious, shot through with subjectivity and based on figures of doubtful authenticity to demonstrate the desirability of projects that, in the medium term, are costly, inflexible and will depress the quality of public services, accelerate privatisation and divert taxpayers' hard-earned cash into the pockets of multinational companies that view the ethos of public service and the existence of the public sector only as a barrier to trade and an obstacle to profit.

One of the most persistent myths is that PFI somehow squares the circle of bringing in new money while reducing the need for scarce public finance that otherwise could not be afforded. That is financial illiteracy raised to an art form. Every penny raised for PFI schools, hospitals and the prisons to which tomorrow's electorates will no doubt commit today's responsible ministers is paid for by the public purse, plus interest, plus profits. Stretching over half a century, in some cases, PFI does not lever in private finance; it merely allows private shareholders to dip their large ladles into an increasing stream of tax revenue.

Independent research shows quite unambiguously that the government could have paid for the whole programme of PFI projects without breaching the sustainable and golden fiscal rules articulated by the Chancellor. The Major government lost control of public borrowing. In a frenzy of creative accounting, they conceived public-private partnerships and involuntarily bequeathed that poisoned chalice to Labour on 1 May 1997.

It is sadness that the government has been so seduced by the flawed and feeble justification for this abandonment of prudence that they have conveyed the firm impression that PFI is the only show in town. Local government and health authorities have trudged down this rocky path with increasingly heavy hearts and increasingly lighter purses.

On value for money, PFI projects cost much more than conventionally funded projects, not least because the private sector borrows at higher rates than the public sector, which is underpinned by the lowest-risk borrower of all: the government. The extra costs are boosted by lengthy negotiations with expensive City lawyers, consultants and fine wines employed by both sides. The escalation of costs is accelerated, notwithstanding the low risks, by the large returns demanded and the ballooning of scale.

The Birmingham schools PFI is a good example. It started in 1996 at £20 million for eight schools and presently stands at £80 million for thirteen schools. The higher levels of finance unsurprisingly lead to an affordability problem for the client authority, which often responds by reducing service and capacity, drives down labour rates and drains subsidies from other budget heads to bridge the PFI gap. PFI hospitals are another example. They have worse staffing levels and, typically, 30 per cent fewer beds.

At the heart of the judgement as to whether PFI provides better value for money than its public-sector comparator is the allocation of risks between the public client and the private deliverer. At this point we enter the seedy world of accountancy massage parlours, where figures are pummelled and distorted into unrealistic shapes. Research shows that calculations of risk are arbitrary and unreliable; what a surprise. A specific example is that the average cost overrun for National Health Service capital projects in the 1990s of 7 per cent can be almost doubled in typical transferred risk calculations to upwards of 12.5 per cent. No wonder that the first PFI hospital at Dartford failed to make projected savings.

Despite frequent assertions by frontbenchers of both main parties, there is little or no evidence that private-sector management, with its hallowed status as a third-way icon, is more efficient at delivering quality services than workers in the public sector.

There is insufficient time to examine the litany of failures. Three will suffice: the fiasco at the Passport Agency, when Siemens paid only £2 million of the £13 million bill; Andersen Consulting's national-insurance recording system, which needed to provide £35 million compensation to pensioners; and PFI's own big daddy – the channel-tunnel rail link, bailed out by a government-bond guarantee that, at a stroke, took back the project's risks.

The belief in the natural superiority of the more creative, innovative and risk-taking private firm over the poor old public authority is seriously flawed. In practice, the private sector relies on the expertise of public-sector professionals to run their newly acquired services. It shies away from too-intensive competition, through takeovers and mergers that have led to a handful of mega-multinationals dominating the sector. Such touching faith in private management flies at the speed of sound into the face of the evidence experienced on a daily basis by those who must endure some contracted-out services in the public sector. Most notoriously, Britain's filthiest hospitals are cleaned, if that is the right word, by private contractors.

My party and my leader seem to take it as read that innovation and the efficiencies of the private sector can be straightforwardly harnessed to deliver public health priorities and goals. However, the fragmentation caused by the PFI approach will divert resources and miss more goals than a Chris Waddle penalty. A key component shoring up the whole PFI edifice is the lowered pay and conditions of staff engaged. High-quality public services need high-quality employment and although transferred staff receive some protection, new ones tend to have poorer pay, weaker conditions and little in the way of occupational pensions. Women, the crucial and undervalued resource in the public services, take the biggest hit. As PFI contracts last for decades, the original tier of staff is steadily replaced by an entire class of women working under weakened conditions and terms. PFI depends on the exploitation of staff. There is a strong link between poor employment practices and poor quality services.

The government states that value for money is the sole issue when PFI projects are assessed against the cost of traditional procurement. That appraisal is heavily shaped by the discounting of future cash flows at 6 per cent. Payments from taxpayers for the capital elements of PFI schemes are typically made later than is the case under conventional procurement. The higher the discount rate used, the better value the PFI project will look in comparison with the public-sector option. Such discounting to a net present cost is flawed in two key ways. First, it does not acknowledge that public-sector purchasing now tends to spread costs over time through borrowing, and the formulaic approach tends to assume a clumping of expenditure in the early years of public sector projects.

Secondly, the real costs of public borrowing have reduced and the arbitrary 6 per cent discount rate used by the Treasury can no longer be justified. Reducing the rate to 5 per cent would make a typical PFI project in this cost area 5 per cent more expensive over its lifetime than its public-sector comparator. That difference is enough to level the spreadsheet in favour of public purchasing for a raft of projects that have been forced down the PFI route. This is not some arcane discussion between sad accountants who should get out more; it really does matter.

In the brave new PFI world, it is not clear that the government have sufficiently strong and flexible mechanisms to guarantee the probity of public expenditure. Politically, PFI and the wider use of public-private partnerships (PPP) restrict the operational terrain for politicians and inhibit our ability to make a difference. Services are supplied increasingly by private bodies that are not accountable in any way that people can recognise. That may lead to a lack of responsiveness by service providers to users, a blame culture between different public bodies and widespread electoral disenchantment.

In responding to today's debate the minister and the government may be tempted to pray in aid the recent publication from the Institute for Public Policy Research entitled 'Building Better Partnerships'. Even that stacked commission felt moved to say that the link between private provision of public services and cost-cutting would have to end, and that partnership should not be seen as privatisation by stealth. It, too, asked that PFI proposals be subjected to a sensitivity analysis to examine whether different assumptions on risk allocation would lead to different value for money conclusions. Even that commission comprehensively demolished the fatuous theory, so frequently articulated in this place by people who should know better, that PFI allows governments to undertake more projects than would otherwise be the case. It does not, cannot and never will.

Sponsors of the commission can in no way be described as politically neutral; they have a direct interest in the expansion of the PFI market and in tapping into public funds for education and health. They have been quick to recognise the possibility of positioning themselves to benefit from the dismantling of the barriers that previously protected the public sector from the warm embrace of private firms.

As the Catalyst Trust said, the IPPR makes the case for extending PFI by setting aside or downplaying the fact that almost all analysis of the potential of PPP acknowledges the inability to improve efficiency, concentrating instead on the benefits of alleged risk transfer.

The methodology used does not take into account the additional risk presented by outsourcing services when the most vulnerable people in our society are the ones who will suffer most if essential services falter or fail and, to quote the intellectual mother of PFI, 'there is no alternative'. Even when risk has been transferred, it has frequently proved impossible to enforce that contract in a practical way. PFI apologists will say that these are just teething problems. My view is that the private sector seems to talk up the risks in contract negotiations but talk them down when raising capital finance from the market.

'Does it matter whether public services are delivered by the private sector?' say the commission, the official position and some of those at the heart of government. Of course it matters. The public sector's motivation is social responsibility, while commercial firms have a responsibility to their owners and shareholders, with obligations to clients and customers some way behind. In countries such as Australia and the United States of America in which health privatisation – by PFI and other means – is further advanced, evidence strongly points towards poorer services with a lower quality of care, more bureaucracy and more inappropriate and less effective treatment. In short, services are down to a price, not up to a standard.

Our party should be the last to stand aside when the necessary modernisation of public services on which millions of our people depend is accompanied by the unnecessary collateral damage inflicted by the PFI: the inflexibility and rigidity of service provision, reduced access, decreased diversity and, ultimately, the failure to meet public need.

We should resist the PFI-inspired erosion of the

foundations of our public services that usher in the expansion of user charges and show the door to the principle of the public funding of services that are free at the point of delivery.

The British Medical Association is concerned that the planning of PFI hospitals presumes increased output because of reduced bed numbers, with attendant implications for clinical services in the hospital as well as for primary care and social services in the community that do not have provision in the contracts. The BMA also points out that an implicit assumption of long-term contracts is that there will be a continued demand for the services of a particular hospital. That pre-empts revenue decisions to be made by local health authorities and primary care trusts for the foreseeable future.

Naturally, the BMA points out that PFI funding is effectively hypothecated and forces resource constraints to focus on staffing. That may lead to unplanned changes in workforce configuration. The non-NHS owners of PFI hospitals will employ former NHS staff, but there has not been guidance to back up the welcome assurance from the top of our party that clinical staff will remain in the NHS. I am unconvinced that that is possible in a PFI context.

In the recent election campaign we were told by the electorate to invest or lose. In yesterday's speech, the Prime Minister told us to reform or bust. Today, we should robustly say that public provision, not privatisation, is the way ahead.

It may be clear that I am opposed to the PFI on accounting, economic, social and political grounds. I remain convinced that public finance and provision remain the most effective, efficient and equitable way in which to modernise our hospitals, schools and other public services. The route that we are pursuing will take us more steeply into a private-sector swamp that is populated by those who set the price of everything but who rate the value of public services as low.

A former Prime Minister criticised a later administration for selling off the family silver. We run the risk of a house clearance of that on which our national family depends. When my children ask me in 2020 – if I am still alive – what I did in Parliament to prevent the disaster of the PFI that will, no doubt, beset them at that time, I shall point to the text of this debate and, I hope, future debates. The PFI is prohibitive in cost, flawed in concept and intolerable in consequences for the taxpayers, citizens and workers who put us in this place and look to us to defend their interests.

Not one paragraph of Paul Boateng's 'answer' to the debate mentioned David's powerful arguments. He concluded with this empty promise:

this has been an important debate and we can all learn from the points that have been made. We make a commitment to the public to deliver better public services and better value for money, with PFI and private-public partnerships being but one aspect of that mission.

I approached Paul Boateng and asked him what his 2012 response to the debate would be. At his request I sent him a copy of the speeches. He replied:

> My recollection is of a typically principled analysis couched lucidly and trenchantly which challenged from a position of authority the then party line. Just the sort of intervention a minister could do without but which one would be best advised to treat with care and respect. I hope I did that but regret that we didn't rethink this when we had the resources to adopt an alternative approach.

David's case was unanswerable. The political class, including the feeble Tory and Lib Dem oppositions, were infatuated by an economic fable that any intelligent ten-year-old child could have seen through. Billions of taxpayers' money has been lost. More will be lost in the future. One of the truths of politics is the unimportance of being right. The foolish prosper: the visionaries are rebuffed.

We wait for the verdict of those who survive until 2020.

SELECT INQUISITION

Unknown and unrecognised but recorded are David's greatest triumphs on the Environment, Food and Rural Affairs Select Committee. His IT background, political convictions, forensic interrogation skills and charm were a lethal combination. He was also an innovator with one daring development that will be imitated beneficially by other select committees.

Select committees are battlegrounds between those experts devoted to concealing the truth and the MP zealots out to reveal it. Usually it is an uneven fight. The witnesses are fully armed with their professional skills and deep knowledge and experience of the topic. MPs are treading on eggshells, feigning expertise on hundreds of subjects often with their protozoan understanding and information.

In contrast to the show business of the Chamber, the select committees are blissful oases of intelligence and calm. The country has been fascinated by the inquiries into 'cash for honours', and 'hackgate'. Twenty-four-hour news has provided platforms for the interrogator MPs who have learned new skills. Select committees in their present form have been in business only since 1979.

Their task is to scrutinise the work of government departments by hearing evidence and taking reports.

Civil servants were once trained with a video on how to give evidence. It advised them to make their answers as long as possible to ensure that MPs cannot ask too many questions. Politicians, captains of industry and other well-heeled witnesses are now professionally coached before they appear. They have undergone dummy sessions with their skilled advisers who have tried to anticipate the questions. They are instructed on the personalities of members to second-guess a likely line of inquiry. Speeches of members are read, blogs and tweets are trawled. Reputations, careers and pensions could be at risk from a poor select-committee performance.

MPs survive with the prepared background information and questions provided by the skilled clerks. Only rarely do MPs shine and outwit witnesses. In two Environment, Food and Rural Affairs (EFRA) inquiries, David dominated a parade of experts who arrived armoured with their stout defensive arguments.

His fellow EFRA committee member David Drew waxes lyrical about David Taylor's skills:

Being an accountant he was brilliant at figures. David dissected the fine impenetrable detail. The witnesses trembled. We investigated the disaster of the delays by the Rural Payments Agency (RPA). The IT firm responsible was Accenture. David took them apart without being rude or aggressive. He was the most pleasant of individuals. But he looked at them and said, 'You

cannot possibly expect us to believe that ... Now tell us
the truth...'

Like all Commons committees the EFRA Select
Committee had strengths and weaknesses. Bets were
regularly placed on how long the Wiltshire MP James
Gray would stay awake. The regular attendees would
also wager on how long it would be before the occasional
attendee Worcester's Daniel Kawczynski would repeat
his tedious plea that the EFRA committee should be
renamed the MAFF (Ministry of Agriculture, Fisheries
and Food) committee to concentrate on agriculture and
not the environment. David Drew fairly comments that
Kawczynski, the UK's tallest MP ever, proves that there
is 'an inverse ratio between intelligence and altitude'.

Witnesses would swagger in, self confident that their
defences could not be broken. David Drew describes
the Taylor interrogation technique as 'like roasting the
witnesses on a spit. Slowly he would turn them gradu-
ally increasing the heat as they went redder and redder.'

If parliamentary oral questions are the sprints,
select committees are the marathons. It is painstaking
protracted work peeling away the layers of the decep-
tion and half-truth to expose the inner core of truth.
Only by preparation, including meticulous background
reading, can a clear penetrating line of questioning
be devised.

David eviscerated the culprits in the mountainously
incompetent Rural Payments Agency (RPA) scandal
where England's farmers had their subsidies delayed

by an overly complex new system. Wales stuck to the status quo and the subsidies were paid on time. David said the RPA was 'poor value for the taxpayer, who is again being asked to pick up the tab because of a failure to properly specify, design and control a major public sector computer development'. Subsidies due to farmers had been delayed in England while Wales adopted a simple system that worked.

David suggested a novel remedy to the immense complexity of the issue. In the Council of Europe he had come across rapporteurs who were appointed by committees to be responsible for collecting evidence and boiling it down in a coherent report for a committee to digest. David teamed up with Lib Dem Roger Williams as joint rapporteurs on RPA. This was an inspired idea and a practical way of dealing with an immensely complex issue, where the truth was buried deeply.

They visited the RPA agency headquarters in Reading and met the staff. David's kind disposition ensured that subsequently he was at pains to absolve the low-paid staff that he met of any blame for the failures. His targets were the overpaid ministers and entrepreneurs who had constructed high barricades to hide their responsibilities for the confusion and delays.

David knew that he had a Herculean task in pinning the blame on the heads of ministers, civil servants and IT specialists. The mistakes were hideous. But, as always, manifest failures had no parents. The faults were those of others or of nobody. It was all just zemblanity. David probed using humour and familiar images to unearth the truth. His irritation and unspoken rage at the preposterous claims being made is illustrated by this exchange:

David Taylor: But he was there for five years and what surprised me about this whole saga is that it is a bit like the poem 'Macavity the Mystery Cat', that whatever happens he is not there, and yet I would have expected that he would have been at the core of what was happening. Were you satisfied with his performance?

Mr McNeill: Alan sat on the RPA Executive Board, he was an RPA director, and he would input. As Hugh would talk about it from an operations perspective and Simon would talk about it from a programme management perspective, so Alan would talk about the IT consequences and what they meant.

David Taylor: So Alan would have said, 'Johnson, it is do-able'?

Mr McNeill: Yes.

David Taylor: 'Tough but do-able.'

Mr McNeill: Absolutely.

David Taylor: Do-able meaning a non-zero prospect of it happening. It could be vanishingly small but it is do-able.

Mr McNeill: The question was, 'As we now stand with our understanding of this, is this do-able?' and the answer round that table unanimously was, 'This is do-able.' On that basis I did not discount it as an SRO saying, 'This is not possible.'

David Taylor: I am surprised he lasted five years.

The defensive obfuscation of witnesses can tempt saints into fury or rank discourtesy. It is sometimes the only way to penetrate their defences. David was incapable of discourtesy and had infinite patience:

> David Taylor: Mr Holmes, which of today's triumvirate have been with Accenture throughout the whole process from 2003? Any of you or all of you?
>
> Mr Holmes: Just myself.
>
> David Taylor: Who has had the greatest opportunity or indeed the responsibility allocated to them for the day-to-day involvement with the emerging system? Would that be Mr Naish?
>
> Mr Holmes: Today it is Andy.
>
> David Taylor: When did Mr Naish join the company?
>
> Mr Naish: I joined the company in October 1987.
>
> David Taylor: You have been with Accenture through the whole period then?
>
> Mr Naish: Yes but I have not had responsibility for the...
>
> David Taylor: I asked Mr Holmes which of the three of you has been with Accenture through the whole thing.
>
> Mr Holmes: All three of us have been.

His questions are models of controlled fury hammering at a cliff of incompetence, complacency and contrived confusion:

> David Taylor: In a sense this select-committee inquiry is a paternity test on failure in relation to the SPS IT

system. Do you expect to come out largely unscathed from this process?

Mr Holmes: We do not have expectations of the end of this process.

David Taylor: Would you accept that your association with this project, which has failed in the most public and spectacular way, will not exactly and necessarily burnish your reputation when you are bidding for future public sector contracts?

Mr Holmes: No, I would not accept that; we do not believe that.

David Taylor: Your part of the project seems to have failed in an unexpected and unpredicted way; the patient had died even though every part of the operation had been successful. Is that how you read it?

Perhaps one day a student of politics can study David's work on select committees. It could be the basis of a first-class primer to all the lazy unambitious MPs who rarely fulfil their duty to undermine self-serving incompetence. Sadly, underperformance by MPs is routine on select committees.

PLOT FLOP

David was troubled about the fate of the Labour government and the party.

He spoke as the fearless conscience of the party when he called for Tony Blair to go in 2005 because of Blair's guilt in leading the country into an avoidable war. By August 2008 there was a new anxiety.

Two habitués of the Peter Pike table called for Gordon Brown's resignation. Gordon Prentice and I were frightened that the Labour government was about to do a 'Michael Foot'. In 1983 the party stayed loyal to the doomed Michael Foot for reasons of affection. The heart ruled the head and an already lost election fell into a disaster. We then had a leader who was less popular than the party. We still had one in 2008.

The Times reported:

> One of Gordon Brown's toughest opponents in the House of Commons – North West Leicestershire maverick MP David Taylor – says talk of the Prime Minister's political obituary is 'premature'.
>
> The member – one of only a handful of hardliners who refused to nominate Gordon Brown for leader when Tony Blair walked away from 10 Downing Street

– believes talk of the Prime Minister standing down and reshuffles as 'we go into the parliamentary summer recess' is no good for anybody. His 'cool it' message comes as one of his closest political allies – Pendle rebel MP Gordon Prentice – has called for Gordon Brown to quit. Mr Prentice was the first to break ranks and demand the PM's resignation. He said:

> I hope Gordon Brown reflects on things during August and accepts that it is in the party's best interests, and perhaps his own, for him to stand down. I want to see an open leadership election where the bar, in terms of nominations, is not set so high so as to exclude credible candidates.
>
> A prime minister must be able to communicate, persuade and enthuse. Politics is a rough old business. You have got to be able to motivate people and I do not think Gordon has those skills.
>
> I just think we need a new leader. Someone has got to speak out.

Gordon Prentice was right. Labour was heading for another self-inflicted wound. The nasty party has always been clinically efficient in dispatching discredited leaders. The nice party sentimentally hang on to old comrades out of misplaced loyalty.

David, Gordon Prentice, Kelvin Hopkins and I had been in the small group of fewer than thirty MPs who did not nominate Gordon Brown as leader of the party.

We were again in a small minority seeking his exit. The party chickened out on the only chance to elect a new leader. The faint-hearted on the front and back benches triumphed and led the party to certain defeat under Gordon Brown. David was deeply disillusioned by Gordon Brown's clumsy incompetence on the unfair politically lethal 10p tax fiasco. He came to regret his reluctance to join the 2008 plot.

On another issue in 2008 the usually surefooted David found himself isolated from his Commons colleagues. He was a lone voice calling for the publication of MPs' addresses.

The Times claimed that:

> The House of Commons stood accused of mounting a shameless cover-up operation to prevent voters from discovering the full truth about their lavish expenses. MPs from all the three main parties were this week bemused to learn what had been agreed in their name.

I had long argued that MPs' home addresses should remain hidden. There was a powerful argument that the general location should be made public to expose those who had committed the sin against the Holy Ghost and flipped their homes. But there were genuine objections to publishing precise addresses.

As the self-appointed adviser to MPs I have preached that:

> concealing a home address is entirely legitimate. Even

MPs are entitled to reasonable privacy. Their families certainly are. If the address is well known, constituents will call in at any hour of the day. It is not much fun when the neighbourhood arsonist, rapist or weirdo drops in for a chat late at night. Even less amusing is when the call occurs during the week when the MP is in London and the spouse and children are home alone.

If the home address is well known before the election, there is one choice only – move. Then never tell anyone the new address. Almost daily there will be requests for details of the new home. Many are from people who are late sending mail, trying to steal an extra day in the queue for action. Always refuse. They can gain time by e-mailing.

There is a serious security risk. MPs are still liable to receive letter bombs or other offensive objects from a range of zealots. At Westminster, mail is screened. Complaining constituents are often angry and violent, as Benefits Agency staff testify by insisting on grills and anonymous name badges.

One sobering incident involved my wife. She was alone at home in the evening and a caller arrived complaining that he had been falsely accused of rape 'again'. Perhaps rural Heather did not suffer the risks of urban constituencies.

Fearless as always, David told the Commons: 'People have a right to know that MPs live in their constituency. Like many MPs, I am in the phone book and I welcome constituents who turn up at my address.'

The Times disregarded the serious hazard especially to female MPs. Some MPs may have been hiding their details to avoid expenses scandals. That is not excusable. But there remained sound reasons for keeping details of home addresses private. The public mood, for understandable reasons, was conditioned to believe the most damaging explanation of MPs' motives. On this they and David were wrong.

STANDING DOWN

I t's a rare decision for a sitting MP to abandon a winnable seat and a meal ticket for life. In 2007 David told his family, staff and friends that he was going to give up the job. He waited until 13 May 2008 until he announced formally his decision to his constituency party in Coalville.

The media jumped to the wrong conclusion with headlines reading, 'Death-threat MP stands down'. David confirmed that he had faced an increase of abuse from his constituents and in some cases threats to his life. One racially offensive comment upset one of his staff and she reported it to the police. David talked of his 'dismay' at the threats. But the main reason for his decision was the 'excessive workload' plus the attraction of spending more time with his family, especially his grandchildren.

He made the conventional genuflection to his constituents:

It's an enormous privilege to have been selected by my party as its parliamentary candidate for my life-time home area on five occasions and to have been able to represent it at Westminster since 1997.

It was no surprise to his party members who were irritated by the delay in an announcement that everyone knew was coming. It baffled his closest friends in the Commons especially those who had small majorities that could be wiped out in the 2010 election. He failed to convince us that his decision was rational. He was the best backbench MP at the peak of his ability and experience. His exceptional local popularity probably made him invincible in his seat. Not that our entreaties moved him in any way. Something else was happening.

One of the constituency papers carried a special section of letters under the title 'The best Man about the House we've ever had':

> It will take a big man to fill his shoes. I asked him to send me some information once. I gave him my name and address. But he didn't write it down so I thought he'd forget. But three days later I received the information I needed. That is the greatness of the man.
> *Christine Smith*

> Thanks for voting against the executive concerning the invasion of Iraq, you spoke for many thousands of ordinary men and women. I have sought your help on a few occasions, I shall always be grateful to you.
> *Barry Fern*

One was canny praise from Andrew Bridgen who was to succeed David in 2010:

Upon hearing David Taylor MP will be standing down at the next general election, I would like to commend him for his commitment to the district. David Taylor has been a fantastic MP for North West Leicestershire, and I admire the commitment and work he has done for the electorate.

David found these spontaneous expressions of appreciation of his work touching and disturbing. Had he done the right thing?

Canon David Jennings spoke of the influence of David's 'feelings of gloom':

Unless you actually talked to him you wouldn't know how deep that was. People like me are trained to probe a little bit. That's what we do. In the conversation we had I knew the disillusionment was really very deep. Very deep. And in fact I even think that if the disillusionment wasn't so deep and if it wasn't for the fact that he had this minor heart worry and if it wasn't for the fact that he had grandchildren, he might have stood again.

A member of David's staff said:

He was tired. He couldn't hack it. I think he was always overwhelmed from the day he got here, because if you're in this job then people will ask you for anything they can get. You have to have a very highly developed sense of self-preservation and David didn't have any sense of self-preservation!

He did a lot of work about mental health, and mental health of MPs. It can be a very lonely job. I was never quite convinced that he wasn't depressed most of the time that I knew him. Not that he wasn't happy, because he was always joyous. But he set rules for himself that he couldn't live up to. And I think that contributed a lot. He felt his principles were the most important thing and if he didn't have those then he wouldn't be anybody.

Pamela is uncertain. She confirmed that David thought of standing down before the 2005 election. But it's still mystifying. Why did he say he was going to give up at the age of sixty-one? It was not a clear-cut decision and he long fretted on whether or not it was the best thing to do. Pamela said:

I still believe that if he stood again in 2010 he might have won the seat again. It was puzzling. The work did suit him but it also got him down. He enjoyed the job but he did work too hard. When he got home he was exhausted. He didn't like to say no to anyone.

His daughter Jessica told me that while working as an MP he had kept a handful of accountancy clients. 'He had planned to expand the business after he stood down and I was going to do some consultancy work for him,' she said. 'He was not standing down to retire; I think that he would still have been as busy as ever.'

Pamela told me he had a few minor health worries with some irregular heartbeats; he had all the tests that showed slightly high blood pressure. He continued his lifelong healthy living by cutting out caffeine altogether.

The Westminster family was intrigued when Tony Blair blamed his own heart problems on the almost hourly injections of caffeine served to him in small cups of concentrated coffee at a European conference. On his return to London, Blair collapsed. His messianic image was still potent. When he blamed caffeine, hundreds of his acolytes agreed. David took statins to keep his cholesterol low. So do millions of others at his age.

In 2007 he confessed in *NuNews* that for twenty-five years he had suffered from the chronic complaint of tinnitus, a ringing or buzzing in the ears. He offered his 'profound sympathy' to the millions of fellow sufferers. He described it as a blight on lives and joined the Board of the British Tinnitus Association to seek practical remedies.

I was unaware of his problem but I recall that he was careful to sit in certain positions at the Peter Pike table to hear the chat. He appeared to be very healthy and was never absent from the Commons. The universal view of family and friends was that he was no more likely to have a heart attack than anyone else of his age.

YEAR OF PURGATORY

David looked forward to 2009. He still had lingering regrets about standing down but enjoyed an energising hope of liberation. He would miss the Commons that he had come to love and that had come to love him. His self-imposed workload had overwhelmed him. He was failing to do the impossible and live up to his own elevated idealised standards. There was consolation in the prospect of liberation from the parliamentary treadmill.

Life was to become more sedate and manageable. There would be more time with his growing family, some light work on local councils and some self-indulgent days at Sheringham. The screaming nightmare of the expenses scandal was a sickening unpredictable menace. It troubled David to the roots of his being. He was not alone. There was group guilt that the community of legislators had tolerated and benefited from a system that invited abuse. We were all in this together.

Probably absent from his thoughts was the prospect of his final demise. He was trim, fit and he lived a robustly healthy life. He had a few minor health concerns about blood pressure that were routine for a person of his age. He took medical advice and lived a healthy lifestyle and ate a healthy diet. His final chance to build on his legacy as a good MP was in 2009. He approached the year with renewed gusto and dedication.

In January there was a chance to demonstrate his now secure independence. What did he have to lose anymore? The Whips' threats were empty. His constituency party was devoted to him; so were his constituents. A new candidate, Ross Wilmott, had been selected to fight his seat. Freedom!

Ross was the successful victor among the twenty-seven candidates who hoped to stand for Labour in North West Leicestershire. Originally from Ibstock, a village a mile and a half from Heather, Ross said that if he won the election he would quit as leader of Leicester Council.

David and Ross had been friends for many years. They were both members of a crack quiz team that excelled in contests on Radio Leicester. David is remembered as a mathematical whizz-kid. He had a remarkable mind. Alan Costello verified his memory for complex canvassed facts that he never 'wrote down' and Pamela recalls his infallible memory of the details of maps. Seen once: never forgotten. He had that rarity of a phenomenal photographic memory which was confirmed by constituents surprised that he did not write down details but replied promptly and accurately.

A hot issue in January 2009 was the planned development at Heathrow Airport. David was one of only twenty-eight Labour MPs who backed a Tory motion calling on the government to rethink plans for a third

runway, which was defeated by nineteen votes following a six-hour Commons debate. As always he never
rebelled lightly. He said he was 'very sorry' to have voted
against his own party and had not done so 'in a cavalier
fashion' but only after much thought and a lengthy
discussion with the Transport Secretary, Geoff Hoon.

However, he had concluded that the controversial
scheme – now a key battleground for 'green' groups –
would be 'an utter disaster environmentally' by blighting
the lives of hundreds of thousands of west Londoners and
damaging efforts to limit the impact of climate change.
He said, 'People are entitled to have their flights to Spain
or wherever, but what we've got to do is contain the
growth of aviation otherwise the impact on the planet
that we are leaving to our children will be very damaging.'

He said more effort was needed to limit unnecessary short-haul flights taken by, for example, business
people who could instead conduct their affairs by video-
conferencing or by using an improved rail network to
travel to meetings.

This was the perfect David Taylor issue: a threat to
the environment, an airport neighbour nuisance and a
wasteful mode of transport. His own neurotic aversion
to flying may have been an additional factor but not the
main one. Only once in his life had he flown. It was an
unavoidable ordeal forced on him when he was included
in a council group visiting Scotland. It was part of his job
to go along with the travel arrangements that others had
made. Pamela recalls that he remembered the experience
with horror and vowed to never repeat it.

During his years attending Council of Europe meetings in Paris and Strasbourg, and on his many holidays in France, he travelled only by road or rail. His daughter Jessica reveals it was not just a fear of flying. She writes:

> He had a fear of heights. He did not like the fact that he had a failing. When we went to Paris in 1989, we naturally wanted to go up the Eiffel Tower. Initially he said he would come to the second level, and then he said he would just come to the first level. When the time came to go up he could not face it at all and instead waited at the bottom with our bags while the rest of the family went to the top.

In opposing cheap flights he knew he was on dangerous ground. To cushion himself from criticism he explained his anti-flying stance. Affectionately he recalled his teenage years when day trips were the full extent of the holidays on offer:

> No fortnights under a Mediterranean sun or even a pale British imitation, just the choir outing to the coast or the Church one to Wicksteed Park. We did like to be beside the seaside and Skegness was the main focal point for many day-trippers and holidaymakers from this area. I certainly have happy memories of the place – the ubiquitous Jolly Fisherman, the Clock Tower (smaller but more ornate than Coalville's war memorial), the Guinness Toucan Clock, donkeys on the sands, sticks of rock, the pier and lots more besides.

No one wants to deny people their hard-earned holidays, but there is concern that if numbers of foreign flights continue to soar unchecked, it is our children and their children who will get much more than a postcard and a t-shirt as the spectre of global warming continues to haunt our ever-more polluted planet.

Leading by example and not just exhortation he told his constituents, 'I'm planning a week in North Norfolk in my last summer recess as an MP.'

Sheringham was the virtuous modest environmentally acceptable alternative to foreign jaunts. David was still devoted to other modes of transport. There was no sign of any slowing up in his strenuous physical activities of cycling and walking.

A month before the exposure of MPs' detailed claims, David had a welcome boost of ephemeral absolution from the worst guilt to come. He was named in the top ten of a 'value for money' league table organised by the *Sunday Telegraph*. It showed which MPs worked hardest for the public, compared with the amount of money they spent and the expenses they claimed. David was ranked equal seventh out of 592 MPs on the list.

David did not stint on the money that he paid to his splendid staff. This lofted his total spending to a dangerous level in public approbation. According to the table, he spent £154,277 in 2007/8, 75 per cent of which was on his staff and office. The alternative is to short-change staff with low wages in order to seek flattering headlines as a low spender.

During that year, his attendance rate in the House of Commons was 87 per cent. He spoke in 225 debates and tabled 197 written questions. As spending, even legitimate spending, was a negative factor, David would possibly have been ranked first had he not paid his staff fairly. A relieved David said:

> It's nice to be named as one of the good guys on this controversial and very thorny issue. I've said before that classifying everything as expenses can be misleading as this includes providing offices in Coalville and Westminster and employing staff to help me to run them. I simply couldn't cope single-handedly with the growing and massive workload of casework, correspondence and campaigns. The pressure of needing to work very long hours to make any impression on a backlog is one reason I am having to stand down at the next general election.

It was a worthy reason for David. Only a handful of MPs judged overwhelming overwork to be a career terminator. The role has no job description. It is up to MPs to adjust their workload to tolerable levels. David's extraordinary workload has been a continuing jaw-dropping revelation to me in writing this book. I have waded through detailed accounts of his packed diaries in a constant state of surprise and admiration. It was self-imposed, excessive and ultimately lethal.

Some of his newspaper columns listed his weekly diary. Although I flatter myself that I am a conscientious workaholic MP I gasp in astonishment at his perpetual commitments.

In 2009 he wrote:

> During the autumn and winter terms, I'm aiming to complete a programme of visits to all of our local primary schools and most secondary ones too. These visits enable me to look, listen and learn so I can feed back to the Secretary of State and senior civil servants on how things are going and the practical impact of educational policies in our schools here in a typical middle England mixed urban and rural constituency.

Most MPs enjoy visiting schools. David's avuncular charm provided an immediate rapport. If the weather was good, David revealed the little known fact that on a few days a year each MP can decide what the weather will be like. Obviously he had insisted on endless sunshine for his visit of that day. It was probably a useful lesson to the children to NOT believe everything a politician tells them.

Visiting every primary school is an exhausting task that no other MP I know ever attempted. Most MPs regard Sunday as a sacrosanct work-free day. It's the glorious oasis of the week when we can relax and wallow in the bliss of family life. My Sundays are precious for the midday family meals, for enjoying my ever-growing family of seven grandchildren. Live media demands occasionally encroach on the early part of the day but

Sunday meal times are never sacrificed. David listed four major engagements on the Sabbath after an exhausting litany of work during the previous six days. Phew!

David was trying to climb a mountain that perpetually grew higher and steeper.

JUDGEMENT DAY

The storm of the expenses scandal broke in July 2009.

The Commons was about to be publicly shamed, ridiculed and reviled. Careers would be ruined and reputations trashed in months of a great screaming nightmare. The venial and mortal sins were anticipated and described but no names had been attached to the sinners. Hundreds of MPs were on the brink of disgrace and humiliation. Few MPs anticipated the depths of the scandals.

David suffered an agony of self-examination. He looked anew at all his claims from the perspective of the average constituent. He was shocked by his own conclusions. He tried damage limitation.

In May, David prepared his constituents for the worst via his website:

> Well, let me begin by telling you what you won't find. For a start, I have never 'flipped' homes. My main home – where I live with my wife and where we've brought up our family – has always been in my home village of Heather. There are no claims for this home.

When I was first elected as your MP, I initially rented in Pimlico until I found somewhere suitable to buy south of the river in Lambeth. When I sold this in 2006, I did make a capital gain and paid capital gains tax – the rest of the money going towards my current flat which is in a more secure and convenient area for Westminster. I have claimed things like council tax, estate service charges, utility bills, furniture and fittings.

When I am no longer an MP and have no need of them, it is only right that I should return the whole value of permanent items to the public purse. If the new consensus is that furniture should be no longer claimed for, I have no problem in making that refund – based on the full-funded purchase price.

I have also received help towards acquiring the flat – interest on the mortgage (but not money towards the capital), legal costs and stamp duty on the purchase. Again, on the eventual sale of the flat on my leaving Parliament, I have always planned to repay the two latter sums from the receipts – after any capital gains tax and repayment of the outstanding mortgage.

He could have saved his explanation. No one was listening. The mob was deafened, baying for blood. It was the summer of unreason when the innocent were accused along with the cynical and greedy. Any defence of legitimate expenses incited more derision. Silence was the wisest course. Anything else fed the beast of excoriating publicity. David was genuinely penitent.

David foresaw two consequences of the scandal:

Wherever this on-going crisis takes us, I have two hopes. One – that we do not come up with a system that effectively excludes many ordinary people from growing up to represent their home area as its MP. We must not allow Parliament to be the sole-preserve of the well connected. Two – that a public backlash against all representatives of mainstream political parties at the forthcoming European and county elections does not result in backing by default for extreme parties.

A ferment of guilt and fear infected the Commons. David was the object of sympathy. A telling sign was his reluctance to discuss the subject. His hands would shake at the mention of expenses. I recall a conversation with him. He explained that he had repaid £8,000 and said there was 'more to come'. That was the total he had claimed in second-home expenses since 2004. The list included new kitchen cupboards and shelves for £2,280, a £100-weekly food allowance when he was in Westminster, his television licence, an £800 TV and set-top box, three rugs totalling £900, a £1,200 bed, a £215 DVD player and £240 worth of pictures.

He also claimed for a £1,500 chair but this was deemed too expensive and was knocked down to £995. A claim for a £347 footstool was struck off by the Fees Office as being too extravagant.

David's explanation of the overpriced chair describes how the ramshackle system worked:

When I bought items for the flat I did so in good faith, in the full understanding that, if any items cost more than the maximum level allowed then I would pay the required additional amounts – which is what I did.

On reflection he recognised the judgement of public opinion with full penitence:

All amounts received were within a framework now seen to have been too flexible and costly – which is why I strongly backed the interim changes announced last week in Parliament. There are now immediate exclusions of such things as furniture and related items, stamp duty and legal costs.

With hindsight the scheme has long needed such major reforms and so I am, in my own case, effectively backdating these changes as a matter of principle. I feel it right to return to the taxpayer all amounts received under these particular headings from 2004 to date. That amount will exceed £8,000 over that five-year period, not including the stamp duty and legal costs which will be returned when the flat is sold after the general election.

I believe David was alone in punishing himself by retrospectively applying the strictures of 2009 to his legitimate spending since 2004. He established the morality of his principle at a high price. He fully recognised the full horror of Parliament's worst scandal in two centuries. Never at any time was he asked to repay any amount. No one was asked to, or volunteered to, repay sums going back to 2004.

He said the expenses row had:

seriously damaged the public image of the main UK political parties and some of their representatives. Personally, I shall try to work as hard as I possibly can in the months leading to the general election to continue to represent this area to the best of my ability at Westminster – an objective I have tried to deliver since 1997.

This was an open, full and brave confession. The money he repaid and promised to repay when he retired was excessively punitive. No other MP made any similar offer. But David did not suspect that there was worse to come.

There was surprising support from an unexpected quarter. The Conservative prospective parliamentary candidate, Andrew Bridgen blogged:

David Taylor has volunteered to pay back some of the money and also to pay back more once he has retired and sold his home in London. David has worked hard as the elected representative of our constituency, but that does not excuse the abuse of an expenses system, which he himself describes as too generous and too flexible.

While I disagree and oppose David Taylor on many political policies, ideology and the record of the Labour government he has been a part of for the last twelve years, I do think it would be unfair and sad if this political snare in which he has been caught along with so many others is his lasting memory in the minds of the electors.

Not all David's enemies shared future MP Andrew Bridgen's generosity. There was severe criticism of David in the correspondence columns of the local papers. There was even more bighearted appreciation.

In the *Coalville Times* there was measured support from David's old sparring partner Pete Baker:

I'll make a spirited, if possibly misguided defence of my old mate, David Taylor MP. David is perhaps not as innocent as I'd hoped, but he has admitted being involved (in a small way) in the expenses scandal.

However, other than his claiming for a rather expensive (but no doubt superbly comfortable) armchair, and I for one don't begrudge him getting his feet up (after all the cycling and walking that he does for charity) on a comfortable armchair.

He also paid his excess claims back without being called to do so. He had not infringed any rules and no call for any repayment would have been made. As for David's daughter staying in his flat that he'd bought in London – I wouldn't have thought him much of a father if he hadn't allowed her to do that (expenses or no expenses). And any parent who wouldn't have done the same thing would be pretty weird parents.

I hope David found these kind tributes of some comfort. His demeanour worried colleagues. He continued to overwork to compensate for his self-lacerating pangs of guilt. At what cost to his health, we will never know.

There are no indicators suggesting he was aware of the fragility of his health. Wet weather failed to dampen his fund-raising efforts. He braved torrential rain to lead a five-mile walk for charity on Sunday morning in early June. He and the other ramblers raised £175 for Macmillan Cancer Support by walking from Snibston Discovery Park to Kelham Bridge near Ibstock. The local Rambling Club are a hardy lot. Their members included five octogenarians and three nonagenarians! 'It takes more than a bit of rain to discourage seasoned ramblers,' David said.

He also rode in the All Party Parliamentary Bike Ride. 'Encouraging more cycling is a worthwhile objective because it's green, it's healthy, and it's economical,' he said. 'We definitely need more cycle tracks, and also more cycle racks, in central areas, where bikes can be left securely.'

These were worthy examples to set. In retrospect they may have been foolhardy risks to David's unrecognised health and well-being troubles. Even though David had published his full unredacted claims to the *Leicester Mercury* a month before the Commons revealed them, the misery was not over.

The remembered items of the scandal were the small ones. There was public outrage against those who had claimed for dog food, a bathplug, chocolate Father

Christmases and a pile of horse manure. Many of these items were minor national stories but mammoth local ones.

I recall seeing puzzling graffiti on bridges in the Wells area of Somerset at the time of the general election. 'One vote = one bag of horse shit.' The *Daily Telegraph* had reported that David Heathcoat-Amory had claimed £380 over three years on expenses for horse manure. There were more serious charges made and he repaid £29,000. A relative of mine told me that the whole village intended to throw Heathcoat-Amory out because of the brazen cheek of his claim. He was sacked in the election with a 6.1 per cent swing against him. The beneficiary Tessa Munt agrees that he was ruined by his inexplicably rash claims. The *Telegraph* headline read 'MP dumps 550 bags of manure on taxpayer'. It became an irresistible anecdote that was endlessly repeated and embellished. Heathcoat-Amory fled politics.

In David's case, the *Daily Telegraph* prominently blamed him for spending £3 on what they called 'face cream'. David? The *Leicester Mercury* followed with the more accurate headline 'Face wash included in claims list'. It was a £3 flannel tagged on to a long John Lewis bill. David had no recollection of making a claim for it.

When the main scandal broke, David was ahead of the game. The other nine MPs covered by the *Leicester Mercury* led the detailed exposures. David had got his retaliation in first by taking all his claim forms for the previous four years to the *Mercury*'s office. He had suffered sleepless nights. He looked again at his previously routine claims and decided that some were unjustified.

David was deeply upset. As an accountant he understood the flaw in the arguments being offered by other MPs. As a proud upright man he was crushed by the accusations. The system under which MPs were paid expenses had long been accepted. They were the rules and MPs worked within them. It was a slack regime that invited abuse. Some claimed sparingly. Others were greedy. We should have reformed the rotten system ourselves. We were all guilty.

The expenses scandal was a wholly justified exposure of dishonest practices. Credit is due to those who persisted in their campaigns to wrench the truth out of the grasping hands of MPs. It was justice – with rough edges. The guilty were rightly hit. But there was a great deal of collateral damage. David Taylor was one of its least fortunate victims.

FINAL FORTNIGHT

The most savage blow hit David in his final month. In Labour MP Dave Anderson's judgement, David was already in the depths of despair that week. The most serious new accusation arrived out of the blue. David was looking forward to the treasured Christmas break. All his now dispersed and growing family would be together at home for the holiday. The worst effects of the expenses nightmare were beginning to recede. There were only a few months left to shoulder the burden of work that had broken his spirits. But he had been transparent, provided all the information that was necessary and repaid past claims more generously than any other MP. He had handed over his savings of £8,000 as recompense and cashed in an ISA. Surely the nightmare was ending?

I discussed the impact of depression with one of the few psychiatrists that I fully trust, Dorothy Rowe. I have known her for many years and greatly admire her practical common sense and wisdom. She assured me that people do die of depression. I gave her an account of the hell that faced David. She thought his despair could have been a major factor in his demise. A probe into the conclusion of the medical profession shows that a widespread consensus is that unmanaged stress can lead to high blood pressure, arterial damage, irregular heart rhythms and a weakened immune system. For people with heart disease, depression can increase the risk of an adverse cardiac event such as a heart attack or blood clots. David's state of mind may have been a major factor in his final illness. No one will ever know.

Another MP's death was attributed to stress. Robert Adley was a strongly independent Tory MP who was an expert on railways. In a rail revolt by backbenchers he was elected to the chairmanship of the Transport Select Committee. The Whips had carved the choice up and all MPs were instructed to vote for Alan Haselhurst. The committee was charged with reporting the Tory government's planned privatisation of the railways. Adley was an opponent of John Major's plan.

When the committee met to elect their chair, three MPs were nominated – the Whips' choice of Alan Haselhurst, Robert Adley and Peter Bottomley who nominated himself. Adley won and Bottomley amassed one vote. The Whips of both parties were angry.

Under Adley's leadership the Transport Committee delivered a rip-roaring denunciation of privatisation. It remains, in my view, the best select-committee report of the past twenty-five years. Adley was under fierce attack from his own party because the report was about to blow a flagship policy out of the water. Publication was due on a Wednesday. Robert Adley, aged fifty-eight, died the Sunday before of an unexpected heart attack.

When the Commons assembled his successor as the committee's chair, Gwynneth Dunwoody speculated on the cause of his death:

> Those of us who served with Robert Adley on the select committee learned to appreciate his total commitment to transport and his clear view about privatisation. I want to put on record the fact that we believe that the enormous work that he did on the select-committee report and the pressures that were brought to bear on him unfortunately and undoubtedly had some effect.

Although the official Hansard report does not record it, I recall the wordless but noisy resentment from Tory benches. There were many who believed that it was stress that killed Robert Adley.

What is certain is that David's worries increased with a new hammer blow. The *Telegraph* struck again on 12 December 2009, fifteen days before David's untimely death on Boxing Day.

Even though David had put the full details of his flat into the public domain, the *Telegraph* twisted the knife in the wound. They published details of David's purchase of his Pimlico flat in 2005, the fact that his wife was registered there in 2007 and that he and one of his daughters were listed at the property in 2008. The matters had been thoroughly aired before. David believed he had fully answered the accusers.

These details were the result of some serious digging by a *Telegraph* journalist six months after the main expenses revelations. The paper believes that this was diligent journalism to inform the public. It may have had a tragic consequence that nobody anticipated. The story played on the claim that David had delayed declaring his daughter's presence in the flat. David knew that most people, including MPs, were likely to believe the worst interpretation of the new charges.

When asked about the information that the Fees Office possessed, he said:

> They would not have known about my daughter before I put in my offset claim, but I was always going to make a deduction for her. I told them before the expenses investigation started – it was nothing to do with that.
>
> It's only right… as she was living there for the whole of that year, that she should contribute towards the cost of the flat. I let the Fees Office know so that no one could argue in some way that she was being given unfair access.

At worst the accusation was that he failed to charge his daughter a high enough rent. He charged her £250 a month. He was later told the going rate was £500. The new accusations wounded him deeply because it dragged a member of his family into the scandal. The privacy wall he had built to protect his loved ones from press intrusion came tumbling down. The fresh charge churned up the old fears. It was a sickening blow.

One of his daughters was subsequently accosted in a street near his London flat by a presumed reporter who demanded to know if she was David Taylor MP's daughter. She ignored the question. The reporter pursued her, seeking his story. The *Telegraph* had admitted accosting others in similar situations.

The incident added to David's self-punishment. He scourged himself with guilt. He was suffering because he believed he had let down himself, his party and now his family. The new accusation left him feeling exhausted, dispirited and helpless.

David's final week in Parliament was one of frenetic activity even by his own standards of ferocious overwork. Was he trying to contradict the new criticism by proving once again that he was good value for money? Did he have any premonition that this was his last chance to shine? Did he have symptoms of the imminent health collapse that he kept to himself?

Only one isolated story hints at problems he might have had. A friend recalled that he looked ill at the November Remembrance service in 2009. It was the wettest day of the wettest November since 1914. It was claimed that a St John Ambulance man was stationed near David in case he had problems. The friend told him that he was not looking well; perhaps he should not be there in such atrocious conditions. He asked David, 'What the hell are you doing here?' David replied, 'It's my duty.' The occasion was of such significance to him that he filed a tiny fuzzy press picture of himself in the line-up at the Coalville memorial in his final week's collection of press cuttings.

Nothing would have stopped David from attending a constituency event as vital as Remembrance Sunday.

This was also the day of tender family memories, when his father openly wept for his comrades lost in the First World War. It may be that David was silent on warnings of his deteriorating ill health that only he was aware of.

Another old friend recalls bumping into David on Main Street at that time. He had a light-hearted chat with David who said, 'Are you aware of the expenses stuff? I seem to be implicated so I hope you do not think any the less of me.' His anxiety was palpable. The friend told me:

> I rang Pam to ask how he was. She said he feels terrible. I told her to let him know that no one thinks any the less of him. If I were entitled to it I'd have claimed it too. We all knew both Pam and David well. We told them there was nothing to worry about.

At the Peter Pike table we endlessly discussed our uncertain futures but death was not part of any of our expectations. Lynne Jones and David had decided not to stand. Lynne suffered disillusionment and longed for a full unhindered life outside of Parliament. She also had health worries. Gordon Prentice deserved re-election but his chances were being destroyed by an avalanche of Ashcroft-funded propaganda. No one challenged the obvious likelihood that Gordon's defeat was certain. David was unconvincing in his reasons for going. His majority and mine were similar. I was fired up, raring to continue. He was resigned to his regrettable but inevitable demise as a national politician. But the embers of his political fire burst into fresh life in the week 14–17 December.

Two days after the new accusation, David was on his feet in the Commons. At Home Office oral questions he asked one of his signature skilfully crafted questions ending in a penetrating understatement. Half an hour later he was back in the Chamber, claiming that the government had been bewitched by bad science by increasing the mainly futile animal drug trials.

In a contribution the following day he proved that alliteration was an incurable trait: 'Many newspapers, having seen the disillusion, distaste and disgust with MPs among the wider electorate, have suggested a substantial trimming in the number of Members.' At Treasury questions he again posed the maximum possible number of questions. He spoke on an unplanned statement and led an adjournment debate about the boundaries of GP practices.

Paul Goggins recalls that he answered David's final question on a subject close to his heart:

While I welcome the new 'Safer Ageing' strategy, is it not the case that the recent spate of burglaries and attacks on older people in Northern Ireland has had a devastating impact on the individuals affected, and will it not in turn have created a deeper fear of crime across the older population? What practical measures are there in the new plan to reduce that corrosive level of fear?

In these three final days before the Christmas recess David asked a remarkable ten oral questions and initiated a parliamentary debate. He packed into that last week more activity in the Chamber than most MPs manage in three months. As always, his words were authoritative, penetrating and humorous – a splendid swan song to a full constructive parliamentary life.

There were few MPs in the House at the lunchtime when David asked his question to Paul Goggins. Most had already left for their Christmas break. Mike Hancock confirmed David's low spirits:

> I believe I was the last to speak to him in the Commons. He was about to travel home for Christmas when I saw him. He was down. He told me he feared that all the credit for the good work he had done as a councillor and MP would be forgotten by the accusations on his expenses claims.

He could not reverse his decision to stand down. There was now no chance to redeem his reputation with future work. They parted, wishing each other a good break and a happy Christmas.

CHRISTMAS BEREAVEMENT

A statement issued by David Taylor's communications manager Phil Ellis announced his
death in direct prosaic terms on his website on
27 December 2009:

I regret to inform you of the sudden and unexpected
death of David Taylor MP on Boxing Day. David
was enjoying a walk with his family at Calke Abbey
when he suffered a massive heart attack. He was
rushed to the Queen's Hospital, Burton upon Trent,
but they were unable to save him. His widow, Pam,
has paid tribute to the efforts of the ambulance and
hospital staff.

Later, Phil said:

David's staff are all heartbroken – he was so much
more than just an employer. A lot of tears have been
shed since we got the sad news. We know just what an
enormous workload he undertook and the anti-social
hours he put in. Although he was standing down, he
certainly wasn't winding down and didn't want to say
no to anyone – there was always another problem to

solve, a campaign to fight or an event to attend. North
West Leicestershire is a poorer place for his passing.

Pamela and the family resist the explanation that stress
killed David. The family had enjoyed a great Christmas
with all the daughters, their partners and grandchildren.
Their large rambling home was filled with laughter and
Christmas cheer.

The Boxing Day walk through the beautiful grounds of
Calke Abbey was a family tradition. Near the end of the
walk David said he was not feeling well. He told the others
to continue their walk while he had a sit down. Soon they
realised that something was seriously wrong. An ambulance took David to the hospital, where he later died.

I share the family's hope that he died a happy man.
He knew that he had been a supremely resourceful backbencher, a polymath and a unique parliamentary craftsman
who had inspired dozens of successful campaigns. He
was looking forward to many quiet years liberated from
parliamentary duties. He wrote about his prospects:

> Longevity isn't very common in the male line of my
> own family, but I am pleased to say that the female
> side does a bit better. My mother's mother's mother,
> for instance, was just a few weeks off ninety-nine when
> she died in 1964. My mother's father almost made it to
> a century reaching ninety-eight.
>
> I well remember the earlier extensive local press
> publicity when she was into her nineties and her
> favourite national TV personality (Ticknall-based Ted

Moult) had dropped by to see her. Such a great age is more common nowadays and would probably not rate much of a media mention.

His own ailing, heavy-smoking father lived to sixty-nine. David reasonably expected to live at least into his seventies.

His early demise attracted a great deal of media attention – most of it fair. An abiding memory of David is his generosity, much of it unknown and revealed only after his death.

John McDonnell's account of the thousands of pounds David contributed out of his own pocket to keep the Campaign Group solvent was a surprise to other members of the group. Only his staff were aware of many of his secret acts of kindness.

The problems of others weighed very heavily on him. He never developed the detachment that shields most of us from being crushed by the misery of others. A member of his staff told me:

> There were a couple of local people that he knew weren't ever well off; he went to school with a few of them. He would always slip them a tenner. It wasn't every week but it was frequent. He just had a very basic redistributive view of money.

Canon David Jennings said that whenever groups invited David to charity events he often could not attend, he would always send a donation or pay for the dinner he did not eat.

Many MPs shared David's anger at the cheating of
the Farepak victims. The collapse of the savings scheme
robbed some of the poorest people in the land of their
Christmas. They were powerless to defend themselves.
I recall the tears at a public meeting I called for victims
in St Paul's Church in my constituency. Almost all of
them were already struggling in low-paid jobs. They
had done the right thing by saving to give a memorable
Christmas to their families. A major bank had robbed
them. Nothing could be done about it.

David gave a day's pay to each of several victims in
his constituency. It was discreet and secret. Even David's
family was unaware of the cheques he gave under strict
conditions of confidentiality. Nevertheless, they were
not surprised or resentful. They understood David's soft
heart and admirable unselfish generosity. One of his
staff said, 'He never had anything that was his. Anything
that was ostensibly his he sought ways to give away.'

My final memory of him was a meal at the Peter
Pike table two weeks before Christmas. I regret that I
did not prolong our conversation about expenses. My
optimism might have diminished his pessimism. He
repeated a comment he had made before to me that
there would be 'more troubles ahead'. I was unaware
of new *Telegraph* criticism of him. No one on our table
read the *Telegraph*. David was not in the mood to dwell
on his new worries. Christmas was coming.

The least mercenary of MPs was brought down low
by accusations of greed. The portrayal of David as an
unworthy politician is a grotesque lie. It's a consolation

that his ceaseless striving for virtue has ended in rest. Robert Browning asked 'Ah, that a man's reach should exceed his grasp – or what's a heaven for?'

The truth of David Taylor's good example will endure and inspire.

WHO WILL WIND THE CLOCK?

'If you do not have to travel today, stay at home' the weather forecast for 9 January 2010 ominously warned. Snowstorms were expected. The invitation to David's funeral was friendly and courteous but carried a warning that the church was very small. The service was to be broadcast to the churchyard. It was a daunting prospect. Churned-up and upset at the loss of a treasured friend, I longed to share the comfort of the service and a few words and an embrace with his family, friends and my parliamentary colleagues.

Leaden-hearted and braced for an ordeal, I set my satnav for 'Heather' and left in the early morning dark. Driving conditions were atrocious and even frightening when I left the motorway and continued on the narrow roads for rural Leicestershire. I am not the world's most relaxed or skilful driver and the disappearance of the white line in the middle of the road and the road edges under a covering of snow left me disorientated. I had planned my journey to arrive early and claim a seat in the church to avoid the ordeal of standing on my arthritic legs for an hour in a snowstorm.

The village of Heather already had iconic significance in my mind. David frequently drew the image of an archetypical Middle England village of stout yeoman living in semi-rural settled contentment. I was conscious also of his repeated recent lament that the rich working-class mining solidarity was being gentrified to extinction from industrial collapse and outside influences. At first impression it was a pleasant rural backwater with no signs of its disappearing industrial past.

There was a warm welcome and a parking place in the Queens Head pub, which nestles under the slight rise on which the village church of St John's stands. When David's victory was announced in 1997, there was a standing ovation from all the regulars in this pub. Even two hours before the funeral Heather was preparing. The police were on the streets and the church entrance was controlled to admit only the most worthy and deserving. There were more than a hundred MPs present who had sacrificed their precious constituency day and made the long trek to honour David's memory. The large turnout included Speaker Bercow and Labour deputy leader Harriet Harman, who was an inspiration.

The snow was incessant. The church was rapidly filled with carefully selected mourners and hundreds stood in the churchyard and lined Main Street. Those of us who were snugly ensconced in the church were puzzled by the sound of applause as the hearse slowly proceeded down Main Street where David had lived in three homes. The welcome new practice of applauding the dead was an eloquent expression of the warmth of the regard that the people of North West Leicestershire had for their MP. There was applause too as the funeral procession passed through the churchyard to the church's west door. The heavy snow continued to fall.

The crammed congregation was reminded that the church had been a haven and a sanctuary to David for all of his sixty-three years. He had his childhood Christian education there and sang as a choirboy. He was proud of his long adult role as churchwarden. It furnished him with much of his rich musical and religious hinterland. Only a few weeks earlier he had fulfilled his regular task of climbing the church tower to wind the clock. He frequently spoke in the church. Its fabric, hymns and language were at the core of his DNA. Paying tribute to the North West Leicestershire MP, the Bishop of Leicester RT Rev. Tim Stevens described him as 'honourable, conscientious, committed, hardworking and principled'.

> For all of us who have known David, we have known him to be an exceptional person who did not make enemies and who won the respect and affection of people from all walks of life and different political perspectives. To all of us and many others, especially his close family, his death came as an unspeakable sadness and a shock.

The service included some of David's favourite music that was very precious to him including Rodrigo and Bolton's *Concierto de Aranjuez*, played by the Ibstock Brick Brass Band. The Coalville male voice choir performed the evocative 'Benedictus' from Karl

Jenkins's *The Armed Man*. It is the sublime sound that should delight and soothe all those entering the gates of the Kingdom of Heaven. The reading was from David's own bible and was chosen by the family as it was the one read by David at his mother's funeral:

> 'Let not your heart be troubled; you believe in God, believe also in Me. In My Father's house are many mansions; if it were not so, I would have told you. I go to prepare a place for you. And if I go and prepare a place for you, I will come again and receive you to Myself; that where I am, there you may be also. And where I go you know, and the way you know.' Thomas said to Him, 'Lord, we do not know where You are going, and how can we know the way?' Jesus said to him, 'I am the way, the truth, and the life. No one comes to the Father except through Me.'

Canon David Jennings spoke movingly of his long friendship with David. They shared deep political and religious convictions. Both treasured the achievements their comradeship won. He described David in homely terms as 'a family man' and 'a local lad who had spent his whole life living in Heather'.

Parliamentarians packed the church and stood in the churchyard seemingly indifferent to the snow and wind. Harriet Harman said: 'This has been a fine service for a magnificent man. We are all in shock and really very saddened by his sudden death.' Speaker Bercow added: 'He was an absolute humanitarian and a superb parliamentarian, someone in Parliament for the benefit of others and not himself.'

There were also hundreds of grateful constituents. The *Leicester Mercury* reported that one who attended to pay her last respects was Lillian Tointon, 77, of Ibstock, treasurer to the Ibstock Stroke Club, of which David had been the president. She said: 'I have known him for years and he has been involved in so many things in this area for years and years. We were proud to have him as our MP.' Terry and Suzanne Knot, from Heather, said: 'The service and the huge turnout demonstrated the respect the village had for him. He was a really genuine guy.' They spoke for tens of thousands of David's constituents.

After the service David's widow, his four daughters, their partners and two grandchildren proceeded to the private burial in the churchyard. Pamela wore one of David's trademark red scarves.

David frequently surveyed St John's churchyard from his garden next door. He knew it was to be his future resting place. In one of his columns he recalled Thomas Gray's elegy written in a country churchyard, 'Where the poet muses on the lives of those buried therein and the fact that most were soon forgotten, their talents going unused or unrecognised.' A reference in the funeral service was made to a quote from the film *Ghost*: 'They are only dead when they are forgotten.' On leaving the church, Canon Jennings overheard a churchwarden say, 'Who will wind the clock now?'

The life of the clockwinder who would not say no will be long remembered.

KILLED BY THE *TELEGRAPH*?

'It's the word in the tearoom,' I told Ben Brogan of the *Daily Telegraph* when he called in to my office in September 2011.

Shortly after David's death I invited all MPs to give me their thoughts. Dozens repeated the Commons belief, 'David Taylor was killed by the *Daily Telegraph*.' It was obvious really. We all knew that David was deeply upset by the allegations made. There were many fears expressed that one or other of the accused would take their lives. Strong, well-balanced MPs were falling apart. To a greater extent than in most jobs, pride is the core around which MPs build their self-image. Now many of these long-respected leaders of their local communities felt deeply humiliated. They were dreading returning home to their constituencies. Would they face abuse and catcalls in the streets? Many did. Foul-mouthed yahoos yelled insults and obscenities at them. The deep-dyed guilty and the saintly innocents suffered the same obloquy.

A greatly respected and honourable senior Tory MP told me a demonstrator brandishing handcuffs had harangued him at the Carriage Gates' entrance to the Commons. 'Are you one of the thieves who has been stealing my money?' the protester yelled. 'I'm going to arrest you.' The MP and his distressed wife did their best to ignore the protester. The MP is a person of the utmost probity with an immaculate reputation that puts him above suspicion. No dishonesty was ever alleged in his case. The incident upset him so profoundly that he wept when he told my wife and me about it on the Commons Terrace. He decided to cancel his trip to the social event that he and his wife were about to attend that weekend. He did not defend his safe majority in 2010. The indiscriminate attacks were cruel and unjust.

Ben Brogan uncomfortably dismissed my accusation that the *Telegraph* report was a factor in David's death. 'It was the local papers,' he told me. 'We reported fairly. Some of the locals went over the top.'

There is some truth in that nationally but not in David's case. David's visits to the *Leicester Mercury* in May 2009 were of his own volition; the paper would not have printed the story otherwise because only the *Telegraph* had the leaked files. The journalist involved respected David and agonised over the decision to publish the story. 'I felt tormented writing that story,' he told me. 'I remember saying how awkward I felt but David told me not to feel so, he said he would expect nothing less than for me to do it properly. Typical David, really.'

The *Leicester Mercury* didn't run the story on their front page – though the *Coalville Times* did. 'We didn't want it to look like we were sensationalising it,' the journalist said. '[An editorial accompanying the story] drew a clear distinction between MPs who had claimed for duck houses and silk cushions and flipped their homes, and David Taylor.'

That was as supportive as a decent local paper could be without compromising their duty to tell the truth to their readers.

The tearoom verdict that the *Telegraph* killed David may be due to the politically malicious accusations that the *Telegraph* dished out to Labour MPs. The pilloried MPs fell into four groups. First to be named were the prominent Labour figures. Some were exposed for serious breaches, many for trivial accusations. All MPs were innocent until they were proved to be Labour. Second were the alleged major offenders of all parties. Third were those whose offences were minor. Lastly the exclusive band of expenses angels was commended. David was firmly in the third group. The *Telegraph* accusations were of extravagance on some items of furniture and the face flannel.

One persistent accusation enraged public opinion. It was the charge that MPs profited unfairly on the capital value of their homes. Most MPs believed that they owned their second homes; they had paid all the mortgage capital costs out of their own pockets. I did not get any serious defence from Ben Brogan of why they confused payments made for capital second-housing costs and interest payments. These were subtleties that did not matter to the general public. Their anger was inflamed. The inerasable die was cast. The canard was that all MPs would steal the last penny from their own grannies given half a chance. A shocking scandal had destroyed public trust in the political tribe. Reason and fairness had disappeared. MPs had done bad things. They were all guilty. They had to be punished.

There was no room for the small thin voice of sanity that said that MPs had largely paid for their own second homes. They were theirs to use as they saw fit. Ian Gibson made the point to the Labour internal disciplinary Star Chamber committee that sacked him as a candidate. They were either instructed to do so or were infected by the contagion of panic to crack down on perceived offenders. Ian Gibson was judged and condemned for the crime of having too much space devoted to him by the *Telegraph*. The Star Chamber was as deaf as the public was to the crucial argument that taxpayers paid only the *interest* on mortgages. That is equivalent to paying for rent of a property or a stay in a hotel.

The decision on whether to buy, rent or stay in hotels was the MPs'. They took the risk of winning or losing on appreciation or depreciation. IPSA, the independent body appointed to regulate MPs, insisted that if MPs sell their properties for a larger sum than the original price they must pass the profit back to IPSA. All those who have bought properties since the 2005 peak of prices are likely to sell at a loss. That's tough luck. MPs must suffer the loss. So if property appreciates the taxpayer gains. If property depreciates the MP loses. This is unfair. But it was the understandable unreason of taxpayers bent on seeking retribution. This was the unjust canard that robbed Parliament of one of its best MPs, Ian Gibson.

Ian Gibson made the only protest possible against an unjust judgement by the Labour Star Chamber Court. They did not understand or even listen to Ian's explanation. They were out to victimise him not on the basis of guilt but on the *Daily Telegraph*'s accusation. He honourably resigned and did not contest the by-election. Had he done so the truth may have emerged from the hysteria. Parliament could still be benefiting from his unique contributions.

I raised Ian's case in a meeting of the Parliamentary Labour Party attended by Gordon Brown. All party leaders were in a race to be seen as more anti-sleaze than their fellow leaders. Who would be judged the holiest of them all? Disciplining Ian Gibson was the point when Labour slipped from hasty righteousness into McCarthyite persecution.

When Tory Douglas Carswell MP gave evidence to the Political and Constitutional Reform select committee in 2012, he referred to the Ian Gibson case as an instance of the powerful grandee MPs expelling backbench MPs. To counter voters' sense of impotence at their inability to withdraw MPs who no longer deserve their support, a mechanism will be put in place to 'recall' MPs to face a vote. One of the disgraced MPs in 2011 continued as an MP even after he was convicted.

It was a hateful period. The press stories of the Whips putting some MPs on suicide watch were true. The atmosphere in the Commons was similar to that in a home for depressives. Brian Iddon MP spoke for the majority of MPs:

A dark cloud descended on the place ... we wandered around in a state of shock and horror at what some of our colleagues had been doing. I could not believe it myself. A feeling of distrust came over the place. You could not look people in the eye. Would they be the subject of the next shocking story?

There was a claimed attempted 'suicide' by one MP who, it was reported in the *Daily Mail*, 'jumped in front of an express train at London's Victoria station during the evening rush-hour. He survived after the train passed right over him and he missed the live rail.' He was accused of the venial sin of claiming for furniture that was more expensive than the John Lewis limits. His claims were challenged by Commons officials who told him they would pay only part of them. No MP was aware of the limits on claims. Inevitably most fell foul of the system at some time because the maximum amounts that could be claimed were unknown.

The MP was devastated by the fierce criticism he attracted in his local press. A prominent trusted national figure threatened to challenge him on an 'anti-sleaze' ticket. Later he decided not to do so. 'For some reason the expenses furore hit him much harder than others,' said a close friend. 'He felt humiliated and has been very low for well over six months.'

He subsequently made a full recovery. His case illustrates the random character of the guilt suffered. The dishonest money-grabbing MPs were untroubled by accusations they knew to be accurate and fair. They knew they were crooks. The honest and virtuous were destroyed by minor foibles that undermined their own sense of self-worth. They suffered.

In the 2001–5 parliament, the most egregious conduct of one MP was passed over and forgiven after a verbal apology. Mr Ian Trend had claimed large annual sums for a property that apparently did not exist. He was permitted to quietly disappear from public life.

David's employee, Matt Mulley echoes the strong Westminster consensus, that 'The *Daily Telegraph* killed David Taylor'. He told me:

> Absolutely they killed him, stone dead. Without mercy, without any real understanding of what they were saying, they killed him. What hurt him most, I think, is he tried so hard to convince everyone in the constituency that he was a great guy. That's so easily undone. It takes very little work to write the story that appeared in the *Telegraph*. But it could undo a lifetime's work. It turned on its head all he stood for.
>
> It was lazy journalism, very cheap. David was more hurt than most: often he failed to get perspective, on what was important or whose opinion was valuable. He thought everyone's opinion was important. How will he be remembered? Those who read the stories about him in the *Telegraph* won't remember him. Those who knew him, met him, will not remember what was written in the *Telegraph*. Even the Tories who knew him will remember a fair Labour MP who was respected and loved.

In the book *No Expenses Spared* published by *Telegraph* journalists there is no mention of David Taylor. He was a minnow in a scandal stuffed with gross illegitimately fatted salmon. But his suffering was deep, intense and palpable.

The Labour MP Dave Anderson sent me this very significant comment of David's reaction to the strain of the accusations:

> I recall at the height of the expenses affair I saw him sitting outside of the nurse's room in the House. He looked really unwell and I stopped to ask him if he was OK. He said he felt 'poorly' but he was going in to see the nurse.
>
> Later that same day he came and sat next to me in the Chamber. I enquired about his well-being and he said he was feeling a little better. He then went into telling me that he was feeling under immense strain because he was being pursued by the media because he had 'foolishly' paid £700 for a piece of furniture. He was distraught because he felt that he had let himself down in the eyes of his constituents and that thought appalled him. He was clearly not well. I was gutted. This most honourable of men had been driven to the depths of despair by vultures who were not fit to tie his bootlaces.
>
> Without sounding melodramatic I have often thought since that this great man was a real victim of the expenses scandal.

LIVING MEMORIAL

David was a genuinely modest man with no higher ambition than to do an adequate decent job. He would have been astonished at the reaction to his death. His memory has been honoured in several unique ways.

In the past, bereaved relatives complained about the formal announcements of MPs' deaths in the Commons. They were cold and impersonal, less of a tribute more a statement of a job vacancy.

Speaker John Bercow splendidly disregarded protocol; happily the present Speaker is a trailblazer liberated from the stultifying Commons tradition of ceremonially announcing the deaths of MPs. He paid a heartfelt tribute to David when MPs returned to Westminster after the Christmas recess. John was an admirer of David's work and hailed him as a 'highly assiduous, principled and independent-minded' MP who 'respected the House and was respected by it'.

To murmurs of support from both sides of the Chamber, he added: 'Truly he was a House of Commons man and I'm sure Members on all sides of the House will join with me in mourning the loss of our colleague.'

Many MPs then prefaced their oral questions that followed with touching tributes to David's memory.

A less welcome break with tradition was the ill-judged clamour from Conservatives for an early election, demanded before David was buried. According to parliamentary convention, by-elections are usually held within two or three months of the seat becoming vacant, but there are no specific rules which would force Labour to hold one immediately before the general election which was due in May.

The inevitable loudmouth quote from the Taxpayers' (Taxdodgers'?) Alliance said, 'Now, more than ever, taxpayers need representatives in Westminster standing up for their interests. It would be outrageous if people in Leicestershire North West go without an MP for months on end.' The Alliance should have saved their breath and berated other MPs, less diligent than David, who constantly underserved their constituencies.

The Tories had a strong candidate in waiting. Local businessman Andrew Bridgen, a former local comprehensive pupil and an ex-Royal Marine officer, had been intelligently preparing the ground for a Tory victory.

Labour said it would not be drawn on the likelihood of a by-election out of respect for Mr Taylor's family. The party was also hoping to avoid the distraction and demoralisation of a by-election that was likely to be a Tory gain. David's 4,477 majority looked fragile without David.

There were many precedents for leaving seats vacant for periods up to six months. No by-election was called.

All parties were privately relieved to avoid two elections in four months.

A series of events were held to honour David's memory. Pamela and her family joined volunteers to unveil a plaque bearing his name at the base of a memorial tree planted at the end of Main Street in the village of Heather. It reads, 'This pin oak was planted with love by his family and friends, on the 10 April 2010, in grateful recognition of David's service to his community, the constituency of North West Leicestershire and to The National Forest.' The colour choice marks his political proclivities. The pin oak has lush green foliage that turns to vivid red in autumn.

On 22 August 2010, three events marked the day that would have been his sixty-fourth birthday. More than 120 ramblers joined his family for a memorial walk at Sence Valley Forest Park in Ibstock. David was national chairman of the Ramblers Association. Coalville's representative Ken Storer said, 'It was a wonderful day and we hope a fitting tribute to David's memory.' A collection raised more than £300 for the British Heart Foundation.

Coronet Copse, near his home village of Heather, was renamed David Taylor Wood. National Forest company chief executive Sophie Churchill said: 'It is timely to look with affection at what he meant to his community and to the National Forest.' A handsome sign was unveiled by his grandchildren Naomi and Henry. More accurately it was 'un-scarfed', with the removal of one of David's crimson signature scarves.

A Commons memorial evening was organised by the

All Party Parliamentary Group on Smoking and Health. David was its chairman and had led the parliamentary campaign that made public places in England smoke free. More recently he had helped secure the successful passage of the 2009 Health Bill, which will put an end to cigarette vending machines and put tobacco products out of sight in shops. Taylor was also one of Westminster's leading advocates of plain packaging for tobacco products.

Deborah Arnott, chief executive of ASH said:

> David was a much loved and respected colleague and advocate for public health, fearless in his pursuit of the things he believed in. I hope it can be some consolation for the family to know that David was admired as a man of great honour and a wise and willing adviser to those who sought his help.

A walk in his memory in the National Forest raised £35,000 for the British Heart Foundation to help other people at risk of heart problems. Three more walks of between seven and fourteen miles were held, with a period of silence at the beginning of each. Events officer Carl Jones told me of a sponsored walk at Calke Abbey, where 400 people took part, including dozens of Mr Taylor's constituents.

Wife Pamela expressed her gratitude to all:

> On behalf of myself and the girls, I'd like to say a very sincere thank you to the many, many people and

organisations who have made a contribution or sent a message of condolence. To know that so many people held David in such high regard has been a considerable comfort for us all through these difficult times.

A separate fund raised £3,000 in tribute cash donations in David's memory. A concert and a religious service were also held. One of the walkers, Chandu Shah, said: 'About fifteen years ago David Taylor presented a chess prize to my son and he seemed a very pleasant man. He was a very good MP and we always voted for him.'

The memorial to David lives in the hearts and minds of the tens of thousands who have been touched by his generosity, devotion and friendship.

COMRADES AND FRIENDS

Shortly after the funeral I invited my fellow MPs to comment on the David they knew. There was a warm response that proved David's gregariousness and his inability to make enemies.

Patrick Cormack MP

I could not pretend to know David intimately but I admired him and liked him very much. Where I did see him regularly was at the monthly communion service and breakfast which a group of us began organising way back in 1974 and of which David became a regular attendee from his first entry into the House. He was a very devout man but totally unostentatious about his firm religious convictions and he particularly enjoyed the All Party companionship and camaraderie which the breakfast group provided. We were all deeply distressed at his death and we will always remember the quiet, often whimsical, contributions he made to our discussions. He was always clear in his opinions but never dogmatic in the way that he expressed them.

Anne McIntosh MP

I sat on the EFRA Select Committee with David and

for all that our politics were poles apart, I found him utterly charming and disarming. His contribution to the committee as a regular attendee and in particular his life's work on the National Forest are a lasting testimonial to him.

Joan Walley MP

David was unfailing in his decency, principles, and always took a personal interest in my family, having met my son Tom at Loughborough University. He shone in his commitment to living his life according to his beliefs.

Mark Pritchard MP

David was a great parliamentary champion for advancing animal welfare legislation. As a new entrant in 2005 he was the first Labour MP to back my maiden Ten Minute Rule Bill, which sought (unsuccessfully) to end the sale of endangered animals on the Internet. That Bill was the start of an enduring coalition between us on a wide variety of animal welfare legislation. I suspect his regard for animals was driven by his deep Christian convictions, which, informed by the Psalmist, call on all men, to be 'good custodians' of all animals. In the 2005 Parliament, exploited and endangered animals had few parliamentary advocates, but David was their Lord Chief Justice.

David Drew MP

I best remember David through his membership of the EFRA Select Committee where he was a relentless

questioner and intense antagonist especially where
the words PFI were mentioned! You knew when he
had had enough of the flannel we sometimes get from
select committee witnesses, as he would turn his 'deaf'
tinnitus ear in their direction!

Ross Willmott
(Labour candidate selected to succeed David.)
I've known David for more than thirty-five years. He
gave me my first Labour Party membership card in 1972.
Ever since, he has been a friend, mentor and a guide.
I've been campaigning for a year and the most common
thing I've heard on the doorstep is that David's was a
massive pair of shoes to fill.

Shona McIsaac MP
Both David and I shared a serious fear of flying. While
others would talk of the trips they had made to far flung
parts of the world, neither of us could be bought off
by the Whips with promises of all-party fact-finding
missions to suss out the beaches in the Bahamas or
whatever trinket was dangled before us. Of course, we
were also firm believers in holidaying at home or close
to home. And we probably had the lowest carbon foot-
prints of any MPs.

Kali Mountford MP
He had a great fondness for walking and waterways. He
always teased me about my constituency's loveliness
and connections with *Last of the Summer Wine*. He

particularly liked Slaithwaite and Marsden, which he deliberately mispronounced just to tease me further, but really he knew all about the development of our canals and waterways, our towns and villages, and loved the beauty of the hills and valleys. If ever we disagreed about anything we could very quickly put it aside with a quick chuckle about the difference between walking the corridors of power and the green, green valleys. I'll miss him trying to put the Colne Valley into Lancashire and I forgive him even for that because his twinkling eye told me he was teasing. That for me was the essence of David: always ready to have a gentle tease and a chuckle and not too serious; more of us should be like that.

Steve Pound MP

My brother Rufus is a monk at Mt St Bernard Abbey in Coalville, Leicester, within David's constituency. He often told me that the brothers voted for David because he often visited them and never did so with any press or publicity. He was highly intelligent and often stayed at the Abbey far longer than he had planned for, as he was deep in conversation. A most unusual and exceptional man.

Andrew Miller MP

David was one of those members who from time to time defied the Whips. This was always on a point of principle and never with any anger towards the people holding the position he opposed. Like me he was an early bird – in the members' tearoom to devour the morning's papers with a mug of tea. The members' tearoom is the holy of holies, one of the few places where MPs can enjoy the company of their colleagues away from the media gaze. The company was often the same. Tommy, now Lord McAvoy, would be in his corner seat plus any three or four from Derek Twigg, John Spellar, John Healey, Vernon Coaker, David Hanson and myself.

David, usually at his irascible best, having voted against the government or abstained the night before, would be seen in conversation with big Tommy. Never did Tommy express any anger, just a few impenetrable phrases from our man from Rutherglen! When in difficulty, David, who described himself as an ecumenical Anglican, would start the sentence with, 'As one altar boy to another…' Many a time he would seamlessly slip into another topic, usually some obscure debate about angels dancing on pinheads or some such aspect of theological reflection. Tommy, who would no doubt argue that Catholic philosophy is the pursuit of real truth, trying not to get drawn, would try to get back to his other truth, namely the Whips are always right!

Andrew Bridgen MP

He and I could disagree over policy until the cows came home, but he set the gold standard in his performance as a constituency MP and a parliamentarian.

If you cut him in two, North West Leicestershire would be running through him like a stick of rock. He is an impossible act to follow. For the sake of my own well-being and survival I will not attempt to emulate his overworking.

David Hanson MP

I had breakfast most mornings in the tearoom with David – we would chew over the papers as well as the sausages. He would always open the day with the comment, 'How's your Margaret?', having campaigned for my wife Margaret in the 1999 Eddisbury by-election. Some days, with Whips around him and with me as a minister, we would discuss the previous night's votes; there was the odd time David had voted both ways as a principled abstention or against the government – no animosity was shown but gentle banter was. David was always thoughtful in his defence. On one occasion I famously (well in the tearoom at breakfast anyway) stole his breakfast – he had ordered the same as me plus tomato. When his arrived I took it and began eating only to find it was David's. I am to this day still the topic of much ribbing and people are told to mind their breakfast when I come in.

In the Chamber David once asked me if I was pandering to the *Daily Mail*. I gently had to tell him that if I was, it wasn't working! But he had a real drive for rehabilitation and tackling the underlying causes of offending. He pressed hard at every justice questions and later at Home Office questions on these issues that clearly mattered to him

It was a privilege to go to his funeral on a snowy day

in January to see so many people who had come from
near and far to pay their respects

Tam Dalyell

I saw David Taylor in 2006 on a forest project in his
constituency. It immediately became apparent that he
had an excellent rapport with both his constituents
and the local and national forestry community. Quite
simply, he was not only respected, but also loved – yes it
is possible for a politician to be loved – by local people
of many different party allegiances. It was confirmed to
me what a serious and thoughtful socialist he was.

LEGACY OF A
CHRISTIAN SOCIALIST

The example of David's work may continue to influence the stormy political weather. Models are needed if the new Parliament is to restore trust in our battered tottering democracy.

Little has changed since the expenses scandal. Most media still judge politicians to be a debased tribe. The parliamentary stables have been cleansed of many dishonest MPs. Other honourable members were shell shocked out of politics by the virulence of public anger and the collapsed status of the job. The splendid Tory reformer Humfrey Malins agonised over the declining importance of the parliamentarian's role in scrutinising legislation while exposure to wounding accusations persisted. Parliament is poorer without him.

The 36 per cent turnover of MPs did not replace old sleaze with new fresh idealism. Fifteen per cent of the new Tory MPs are from lobbying jobs. Twenty per cent of former MPs have been reincarnated as lobbyists. The essential period of repentance and reform has not happened. New sleaze is emerging. The continuing erosion of trust in democracy has drawn people into the dangerous alternatives of extreme views. Through contagious infantilism blind faith in royalty has been elevated. Despair at the financial crisis has persuaded nations to desert democracy and hand power to technocrats.

David's life may help to foster a restoration of the concept of the honourable member. Dedicating to him my rewritten guide to Parliament, *How to be an MP*, is to acknowledge the devoted idealism and purity of his character. David described his role as trying 'to hold the government to account on behalf of my constituents, and to steer a line between mindless obedience and persistent rebellion'. For that he was honoured by his peers with the only award that MPs value. David knew that he had already achieved the highest accolade a British democrat can aspire to with the letters MP.

He was unfairly dragged into the maelstrom of the Commons expenses scandal. His friends knew that his behaviour was always strictly honourable. Inevitably some of his obituaries were hastily written, Google-derived accounts of recent publicity that had deeply wounded him. Obituaries by Tam Dalyell and other friends identified his abundant virtues. He told a fellow MP a fortnight before his death that he feared the malicious reporting of his expenses claims would eclipse all the good he had done in decades of work as a councillor and an MP. That will not happen.

Tony Wright, in his fine new book *Doing Politics*, describes a call from Tony Blair asking for a definition of socialism. That may explain many of the tensions between the party and Blair. David needed no explanation. He described himself as 'socialist and proud of it'. He instinctively understood his political creed and his Christianity. To him they were parallel inspirations that shaped his life. He was loyal to the core values of the Labour Party. He also described himself as 'typical working class' and a 'mushy peas rather than a guacamole socialist'.

His never-failing courtesy and lack of malice secured the affection of his colleagues. He served his constituency with maternal zeal. David's iconic success and character make him an admirable model for all parliamentarians. His passing has left Parliament bereaved. We all miss his friendship, modesty, his infectious laugh and his never-failing kindness.

British politics is still adrift in the dangerous waters of uncertainty and incipient sleaze. Reforms will come from the determination of backbenchers to question and rebuild.

David Taylor's life is a shining beacon to illuminate the way forward.

INDEX

INDEX